Living
Off the Sea

By Charlie White

Living
Off the Sea

By Charlie White

Technical illustrations by Nelson Dewey
Fish drawings by Chris Sherwood

Canadian Cataloguing in Publication Data

White, Charles, 1925-
  Living off the sea

  ISBN 0-919214-77-0

  1. Seafood gathering - British Columbia.
2. Fishing - British Columbia.   3. Cookery
(Seafood) I. Title. II. Series.
Sh400.8.C3W49 1985   799.1'6   C85-091364-0

HERITAGE HOUSE PUBLISHING COMPANY LTD.
Box 1228, Station A., Surrey, B.C. V3S 2B3   Printed in Canada

*I dedicate this book to
my three sons — Chad, Kevin and David — who
helped me with much of the experimental work.*

About the Author

Charlie White is an internationally known Canadian engineer-cum-biologist, fisherman, author, lecturer and film-maker who has been referred to as the Jacques Cousteau of the salmon fishing world. The life and times of the salmon and how to catch them is his life's work.

He began experimenting with an underwater television camera in 1972, and he devised a unique system which enabled him to study salmon behaviour. He can watch on a television set in his boat while the camera captures the action of his lure and the salmon's reaction to it — a dream come true for any fisherman!

In 1981 Charlie released "Salmon Spectacular", his first full-length feature movie. It received rave notices from major newspapers throughout North America. "In Search of the Ultimate Lure", Charlie's new feature length film, uses the latest underwater camera techniques to detail Charlie's most recent research into fish strike behaviour, and his quest to discover the ultimate lure.

Charlie has written a series of books on marine life which have sold hundreds of thousands of copies, making him one of Canada's most popular outdoor authors. His latest book is *Charlie White's 101 Fishing Secrets*. He has also had articles published in *BC OUTDOORS*, *PACIFIC YACHTING*, and several U.S. publications.

Contents

Foreword

Scientists around the world have been stating for many years that the sea is an almost inexhaustible source of food for mankind. Some have stated flatly that, with proper management, the oceans of the world could feed everyone who will live on this planet for the next thousand years.

This feeling that the sea is the mother lode to feed the human race makes more urgent the warnings that we protect our waters. We are chewing up the arable land for houses, roads, and factories to supply our expanding populations and economies. As we blacktop thousands of acres each year and lose them forever for agriculture, we must be sure that the sea, our last great food generator, is kept pollution free and in good "working" order.

Forming the base of the whole marine food chain are the planktonic organisms. These microscopic plants (phytoplankton) and animals (zooplankton) feed on the minerals and nutrients washed into the sea from the rivers and streams. They also feed on the nitrogen-based nutrients brought up from the very deep water by sweeping vertical currents or upwellings. As these organically rich waters move close to the surface, sunlight acts as the catalyst to allow the plankton to feed, grow and multiply.

Small shrimp-like organisms called euphasids gobble up the plankton and set the stage for the next step in the food chain.

Now the smaller fish — herring, anchovies, etc. — move in to feed, with oysters, clams, and other shellfish actively filtering these tiny organisms, converting them into body protein. Some very large fish also feed directly on tiny planktonic or euphasid nutrients. Basking sharks and whale sharks are examples (some over 50 feet in length) of fish which bypass one step in the food chain and go directly to the plankton or euphasids. The largest whales feed in this manner, filtering tons of nutrients each day to supply their gargantuan bodies.

Larger fish — cod, rockfish, salmon, various sharks — let the herring and anchovies do the work of gathering up the food and condensing it in their own bodies (sort of like concentrated orange juice). Then they attack the schools of herring and get their food supply in convenient large amounts.

Crabs and some shrimp also feed on this level of the ocean food chain. They eat clams, other bottom dwellers, and wounded or dying fish and scraps which settle to the bottom. But they are not scavengers in the sense that they do not eat putrefied or rotten food.

This has been a simplified picture of the general operation of the sea's food factory. There are many variations, exceptions and contradictions to the principles described, but it gives a basic idea of what is happening in the food chain ecosystem, struggling for survival under the sea.

Part One

A Sea of Shellfish

Introduction

Fortunate enough to live on a small inlet along the inside of Vancouver Island near Victoria, I can catch enough food any day of the year from the shore or from a small craft to feed my whole family. The sea itself is my refrigerator, keeping everything fresh (and alive) until the moment I need it.

There is plenty of good protein in the sea: Delicacies such as clams, crabs, oysters, sole, flounder, rock-fish, cod, shrimp, prawns, and even various seaweeds. Certainly a steady seafood diet can get tiresome, even the gourmet choices listed above, but it is a reliable supply of excellent protein food.

I have often thought about how I might survive under "disaster" conditions by living off the sea.

There are many books available about how to live off the land, both for a natural eating experience or for wilderness survival. There are several "doomsday books" predicting disaster from atomic fallout, and others predicting world-wide financial chaos.

I found the economic doomsday forecasts more scary! The logic expressed in the books seemed unassailable. Shortages of vital raw materials (oil, metals, food) are definitely possible. Runaway inflation could result, and the economic system could break down leaving each person or family unit to survive on its own.

Various means of getting through the predicted period without an economic system to help supply the necessities of life have been

11

suggested. Hoarding of food, clothing and other vital supplies was the most common. Another suggestion was a "back to the land" approach — growing your own food and meat. This seemed a good way to get fresh food and a healthy outdoor existence, even if doomsday didn't arrive.

The one flaw in this whole scheme, in my opinion, was the mob or panic reaction that was likely to occur during this time. The home gardener or farmer would likely be overrun by others who would simply steal what they needed to survive. A person might keep his hoard quiet, but marauding bands of hungry people might well search all homes and find any cache.

As I thought about how I might survive under such conditions, I realized that living off the sea might be the best answer. Knowledge of how to find and catch the various species is something no mob can take from you. Shovels, hooks, line, crab traps and other bare necessities to catch fish are easier items to hide than a field of vegetables, a chicken, or a cow.

This book is not a survival manual, rather one intended to increase your enjoyment of being on the sea, although the information presented could help you in the event of a disaster. It will help you add variety to your menu at little or no cost after a small investment in equipment. It is a guide for those who wish to tap the wealth of the sea and have a lot of fun at the same time.

Since it is not a doomsday book, I will be suggesting the use of equipment and techniques which cannot be used under primitive conditions, although most can be adapted to more basic techniques. These methods of living off the sea can be applied by most boaters, from the car-topper to the luxury yacht owner.

Some of the basic material in this book is taken from our earlier "How To" paperbacks on catching crabs, shellfish, bottomfish, salmon and cooking your catch. However, the contents have been expanded and updated with the latest information from our underwater research filming techniques.

Good reading, good fishing, good eating ... and good living off the sea!

— *Charlie White*

CHAPTER I
CRABS
AND
CRABBING

Crabs are found in all the oceans of the world, from the giant king crab of the Arctic to many of the subspecies in warm tropical waters. There are many edible varieties, and crabs are considered a true gourmet delicacy almost everywhere. The delicate flavor and texture of crab meat is a prime ingredient in many recipes used by the great chefs of the world.

I often wonder how primitive man first discovered crab meat. It must have taken a lot of courage to kill this fearsome looking creature and eat the very first one.

EDIBLE CRAB SPECIES

The most popular and plentiful crab along the Pacific Coast is the Dungeness crab, or sand crab. Other edible species include the red rock crab, box crab, Alaska king crab, snow crab and Tanner crab or queen crab.

Dungeness Crab

This name is derived from Dungeness Spit, a popular crabbing area on the north side of the Olympic Peninsula in the Strait of Juan de Fuca separating Washington State from B.C. They are also

13

called sand crabs because they are usually found over sandy bottomed areas.

They are the major commercial crab of the Pacific coast from northern California to Alaska. This is the crab cooked in the crab

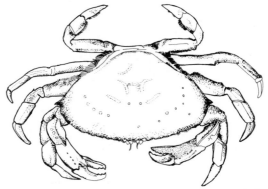

The Dungeness crab is the major commercial crab of the Pacific coast.

pots at Fisherman's Wharf in San Francisco and the major ingredient in crab cocktails, crab Newburg and other popular dishes.

The males can grow to a size of eight to 10 inches across the back of the shell (carapace), but the average commercial size is usually about seven inches or somewhat less. They have large, meaty legs and claws plus an equal amount of body meat in the underside of the shell.

Rock Crab

This crab is found generally over the same area as the Dungeness crab. Normally smaller than the Dungeness crab, it has a very hard, reddish brown shell. It is not taken commercially, but the meat is quite edible. I find it a bit more stringy than Dungeness crab meat, but quite tasty nevertheless.

The legs are mostly small and spindly with very little meat. However, the claws are very large, even larger than Dungeness, and are the major source of the meat in this variety. The body contains very little meat, but with patient cleaning, you can get a good meal from the legs and body of rock crabs.

Box Crabs

These are very colorful crabs, with hard shells covered with spiky horny bumps. They are found in very deep water and are seldom taken in normal crabbing activities. Scuba divers often find them on rocky bottoms.

One variety is called a "decorator crab" because of its habit of attaching colorful bits of seaweed to its shell. When I operated the Undersea Garden tourist attraction in Victoria, we used to put multi-colored confetti in the water near our box crabs and found it fascinating to watch them decorate themselves like Christmas trees.

Box crabs get their name because they fold their legs and claws in against the shell in a neat fit that looks somewhat like a box — almost like a marine Rubik's cube. Some of the larger specimens are erroneously called king crab by local divers, but this is a completely different species from the much larger Alaska king crab.

King Crab

These huge crabs are taken primarily in large traps in deep water off Alaska. There are also local populations along the B.C. coast and in the Queen Charlotte Islands.

As far as I know, there is little or no sport fishing for king crabs, primarily because of the rugged open water areas in which they are found. The same holds true for the other related species of queen crab, snow crab and Tanner crab.

LIFE CYCLE

Crabs come in various shapes and sizes, but all have the characteristic rounded or elliptical outer shell (carapace), a set of claws or pincers, and eight additional jointed legs. These jointed legs put crabs in the same general classification as spiders, shrimps, lobsters, centipedes and the vast insect world. In fact, this is the largest group of animals in the world.

When crab eggs hatch, the tiny babies float freely in the sea in what is known as the larval stage. They are almost microscopic in size and drift in the ocean currents along with plankton and euphasid creatures. The larvae settle to the bottom and after a few weeks have taken on their characteristic adult shape.

In B.C. waters, crab larvae are plentiful during the month of June, and salmon often feed heavily on them. Coho are especially fond of crab larvae and are often difficult to catch on hook and line at this time because no artificial or natural bait looks anything like these larvae.

As crabs feed and grow they have a problem similar to insects and other animals with exoskeletons. Animals higher on the evolutionary scale have internal skeletons to support their body structure; creatures with exoskeletons do not have this advantage. A crab, for instance, can grow only by first "molting" its shell (skeleton) and then growing a new and larger one.

Crabs molt many times in their early life but less often as they mature. Molting begins when a split appears across the rear of the shell. The crab literally backs out of his old shell, leaving behind a complete shell including claws, legs and back. In later spring when there are large numbers of molting crabs, the fisheries department often gets calls from alarmed residents saying there are thousands of dead crabs on the beach. The "dead crabs" are only the empty, molted shells.

At this stage the crab has a butter-soft new skin, and absorbs water which allows it to swell up to a new, larger size. It is protected only by its soft skin, and will usually bury itself in the sand for several days until the new shell begins to harden. The hungry crab then comes out of the sand and feeds very heavily in order to fill out its newly enlarged shell.

Crabs caught during this time have soft shells, with not much meat. The body meat is still quite tasty, although it seems a bit more "watery." The leg and claw meat tends to be mushy and stringy.

Crabs reach a size of about 1¾ inches across the back of the shell during the first year, and are about four inches across after two years. Male crabs are sexually mature after three years and are about six inches across at that point.

Most areas have regulations which prevent capture of male crabs until they reach their fourth year of life. Regulations usually require a width of six inches across the narrow part of the shell, or 6½ inches across the widest "tips." This allows male crabs to mate once before reaching legal size, a sensible regulation, since fisheries department statistics show that more than 95 per cent of legal crabs are taken in many areas each season. If we didn't allow the males one mature season, there would be lots of lonely females out there, and much lower crab populations.

FINDING GOOD CRAB HABITAT

Rock crabs are widely distributed throughout B.C.'s inland waters, in Puget Sound and in bays and inlets all along the coast from Alaska to California. They can be found on almost any kind of bottom including rock, gravel, sand or mud.

Dungeness crabs are generally found on sandy bottoms, especially where there is good tidal action. In inland waters, you can generally find these crabs in sandy bottom areas with eel grass or a sandy area at the mouth of a river or stream. Due to strong tidal movement, there is often good crabbing off a long sandspit, as at Dungeness Bay on the Olympic Peninsula.

There are also large populations of crabs in offshore waters in the open sea. Commercial crabbers get the majority of their catches using large commercial traps set just offshore of the breaking surf in 30 to 50 feet of water. Most are harvested from commercial crab boats, but some are now being taken by helicopters which can hover over the surf to pick up the traps in almost any weather.

Not much is known about the migration patterns of Dungeness crabs, although a series of tagging experiments by fisheries departments in Oregon and Washington is beginning to reveal some data.

Most crabs tend to live out their entire life in a relatively small area, moving back and forth between deep water and shallow water. However, some do move considerable distances. One crab tagged south of Westport, Washington was later recovered in 300 feet of water almost 40 miles away. Some crabs, especially males,

Rock crabs can be found throughout B.C.'s inland waters on almost any kind of bottom.

tend to move offshore into deeper water during the heart of the winter and return inshore during the spring. Biologists speculate that these movements are motivated by a search for food and mates.

Mating takes place in late spring when male and female crabs are found in mating pairs in shallow water. Only after the female has molted can mating occur, but the male will often carry the female clasped to his underside for a month or more waiting for her to molt.

Other crab migrations are dictated by weather conditions. In coastal bays, heavy rainfall and strong river flows will lower water salinity, and the crabs are forced into saltier water offshore.

CATCHING CRABS

The simplest method of catching crabs is to search them out in tidal pools during extremely low tides. They can sometimes be found buried in the sand or hiding under seaweed and other debris. You can find them by poking with a stick or even with your rubber boots. Once prodded out into the open, they can be picked up and placed in a collecting bucket or burlap sack.

Crabs can also be taken during low tides using a scoop or fish landing net. Some people use chest waders and simply walk through shallow areas looking for legal sized males. Others float over these same areas in small dinghies, using polarized sunglasses to help them see through the surface glare. This is a most exciting way to catch crabs. The crabs will usually dart back and forth like an open field football halfback, and it is great sport to try to get the net or scoop under the crab and flip it into the boat.

In late spring you will see the mating pairs mentioned earlier. The male is in prime condition at this time and is relatively easy to catch because of the added burden of carrying a female. The female will sometimes be dropped during the chase, if not you can always release her after catching the male.

Crab Rings

A crab ring is a simple piece of equipment consisting of two wire rings attached together with strong netting and thus forming a collapsible basket. The lower ring is smaller than the upper ring. The bait is tied securely to the bottom of the basket and lowered to the sea floor where the sides collapse, leaving only a flat platform with the bait in the middle. They require frequent attention because the crabs can steal the bait and leave quickly.

After 15 to 30 minutes, the ring is raised rapidly by a rope attached to the sides of the top ring. This holds up the sides of the basket and traps the crab while it is pulled into the boat. The ring must be retrieved quickly and steadily so the water pressure forces the crab against the bottom of the basket and prevents it from climbing over the sides.

Crab Traps

Traps are the most effective method of catching crabs. Commercial operators use this method almost exclusively. The traps range from simple home-made wooden framed models, through collapsible net traps, right up to heavy duty stainless steel models costing $100 or more.

Collapsible traps are usually not as effective as the round fixed models, but are very convenient for use on a small boat where storage space is a major problem. They usually catch enough crabs for a good feed which is the object of the exercise, anyway.

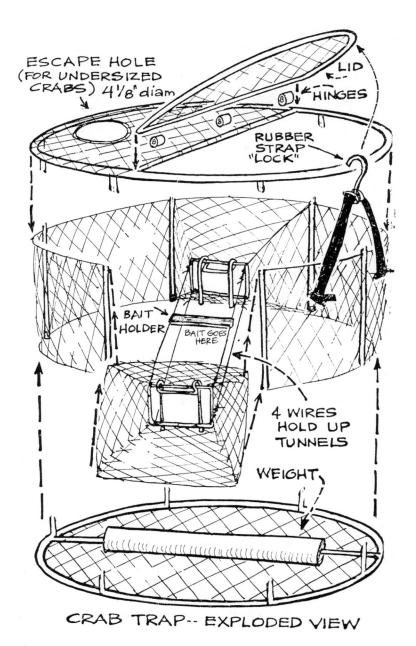

ESCAPE HOLE
(FOR UNDERSIZED
CRABS) 4 1/8" diam

LID

HINGES

RUBBER
STRAP
"LOCK"

BAIT
HOLDER

BAIT GOES
HERE

4 WIRES
HOLD UP
TUNNELS

WEIGHT

CRAB TRAP -- EXPLODED VIEW

The trap used by commercial crabbers has proved effective for a number of reasons:

1. Side Entrance Tunnels — Entrance tunnels on the sides of the trap, sloping up from ground level to make it easier for the crabs to enter. Entrance tunnels on the top of the trap are less effective, since the crab has to detour away from a direct approach to the bait and may have difficulty climbing up over the mesh of the trap. Long entrance tunnels are more effective than short tunnels, since a captured crab tends to work its way around the perimeter of the trap. The long entrance also makes escape more difficult.

2. Round shaped trap — A round trap is more effective than a square or rectangular trap since a hungry crab often will not go around sharp corners. A round trap allows the crab to work its way around a gentle curve to the entrance tunnel.

3. Anti-escape hinge — This is simply one or two pieces of wire hanging from the top of the inner end of the entrance tunnel. The hinge falls back in place after the crab has entered, thus preventing escape.

4. Escape hole — This is a round hole about 4½ inches in diameter which allows undersized crabs to escape. When a large crab enters the trap, the small ones tend to leave quickly, leaving more room for larger crabs. Allowing small crabs to escape saves the bait and also saves the trouble of taking them out of the trap. It is also a good conservation measure, since the small males and females can escape without damage. Escape holes also help get rid of rock crabs, which tend to be very tough and pugnacious in a trap. They also tend to discourage Dungeness from entering the trap.

CRAB BAIT

One of the most prevalent myths about crabs is that they like smelly or rotten baits. I have just finished reading several books on catching crabs in Florida and Louisiana which still advise that rotten baits are productive. However, biologists have made tests which show conclusively that crabs prefer fresh food. They live on clams, marine worms and small fish.

A researcher in Oregon found that rotten baits tended to catch undersized males and females, while larger males will seek fresh food. This is probably because the smaller crabs have difficulty competing for fresh food, and will sometimes accept the less desirable product. Fresh clams, fish carcasses, entrails or fresh flesh from any marine animal are all effective as crab bait.

Some commercial operators use chicken parts (necks, gizzards, entrails) with some success, but non-marine baits have not been as effective for me. I have tried using scraps of beef, pork or bacon in my traps, with poor results.

Flav-r-glo, Inc. of Portland, Oregon is experimenting with an artificial flavored bait for crabbing. These bait wafers are said to release a flavor into the water for two to four hours, and increase catches. However, their tests also show that marine baits outfish non-marine baits such as chicken necks, etc.

My own favorite crab baits are herring, which tends to put a strong attracting oil into the water, and carcasses from Pacific cod (this is the cod with the barbel under its chin). For reasons I do not understand, this flesh is far more effective than either rockfish or ling cod carcasses.

BAIT CUPS

Many crab baits tend to break up and disperse easily in the water which makes them undesirable as crab bait. A bait jar or cup with holes punched in the side and lid is an effective means of holding

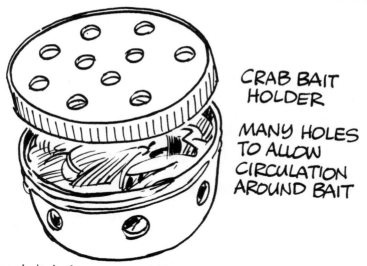

CRAB BAIT HOLDER

MANY HOLES TO ALLOW CIRCULATION AROUND BAIT

these baits in the proper position inside the trap. They are excellent for holding chopped clams, coagulated fish blood, chunks of herring, salmon eggs and fish entrails. Salmon eggs are a wonderful delicacy for crabs.

Using bait jars also will allow the trap to be effective over long periods of time since the smell of the bait will attract the crabs, but does not allow the bait to be eaten. Bait jars can keep a trap fishing productively for several days.

Frozen Bait

After fishing, I clean my salmon or cod and then fillet the meat. This leaves the head, tail, entrails and the main backbone for crab bait. I can then use stove pipe wire, stainless steel wire, or even nylon line to wire together the fish heads and filleted frames before freezing.

These baits are then wrapped in newspaper or a plastic bag and placed in the freezer, all ready to go on my next crabbing trip.

Bait Placement

It is important to place all crab baits or bait jars directly in the center of the trap between the entrance tunnels, and have them wired securely in place. If the baits are thrown loose into the trap, the tide will push them to one corner and the crabs will feed from the outside of the trap. Placing the bait between the entrance tunnels encourages the crab to enter the trap.

How Much Bait

I have done many experiments using small amounts of bait and large quantities of bait in my traps. Invariably, the trap with the largest quantity of bait catches the most crabs. Sometimes the difference is quite dramatic, with four or five times as many crabs in the heavily baited trap. I think this is partly due to the fact that crabs are attracted by sight as well as by smell. They can see the large quantity of bait, and are attracted to it, even with other crabs already in the trap.

SETTING THE TRAP

Local knowledge is extremely important in choosing the precise location for your trap. It is wise to ask local marina operators, outdoor writers and other local outdoorsmen for details on good crabbing spots.

Generally speaking, Dungeness crabs will be found on a sandy bottom in between 15 and 50 feet of water with good tidal movement. If you see the floats from other crab traps, it is probably a good bet to set yours in the same general area. You can also tell something about the bottom by looking on marine charts which indicate whether the bottom is sandy or rocky.

Be very careful in setting the trap that you have enough line to reach the surface. When I first began crabbing, I would excitedly throw my trap over the side and watch the float disappear as the trap plunged into water too deep for my float line. Now I hold onto the line until I am sure the trap is safely on the bottom.

When setting the trap, it is vital to line up the entrance tunnels with the flow of the tide. The Pacific biological station in Nanaimo did some interesting experiments to see how crabs enter a trap.

They used an underwater TV camera mounted above the trap, and observed the crabs as they entered. The crabs approached against the current. Evidently they were picking up the smell of the bait and following it directly to the trap.

When the tunnel entrance was lined up with the current flow, the crabs would walk directly up the tunnel entrance and into the trap. However, if the tunnels were set at 90 degrees to the tidal flow, the crabs would walk back and forth outside the trap, and claw at the trap mesh. Some would work their way around to the tunnel entrance, but others would just wander away. If you line up the tunnel entrances at the surface, then lower the trap on a slack line, you will usually end up with the tunnels properly aligned.

Markers on Crab Floats

It is important to take "gunsight" marks or range markers to locate your floats. Finding your trap in a cluster of others can be difficult.

SPRAY-PAINT WITH 'DAY-GLO' FOR BETTER VISIBILITY

Good floats are needed on crab traps. Use paint on metal bottle caps to prevent rust.

It becomes almost impossible if the wind comes up and the water is a bit choppy. Gunsight marks (line up two objects on shore, one behind the other) will help you get an exact "fix" on your trap float. (See page 87, Positioning Techniques, for full details.)

BEST CRABBING TIMES

When crabs are feeding actively, I check my trap every 45 to 60 minutes and have excellent catches. At other times, it is best to leave the trap overnight for maximum success.

Crabs tend to feed better on a flooding tide than an ebbing tide. However, the best time is at slack tide when there is very little tidal movement. In this regard they are similar to fish who hate to work hard in that it is easier to move around and search for food when there is no current.

My own experience is that high slack tide is the best crabbing time, followed by low slack tide. A small flood tide can also produce good crabbing. Small ebb tides are okay, but fast flowing ebbs or floods are relatively poor. When using bait jars or cups, catches will be increased by leaving the trap overnight.

FLOATS

Since crabbing is often best in areas with good tidal flow, it is important to have a proper float which you can find in strong tidal currents.

Several large floats or bleach bottles can overcome the currents and hold them at the surface. If you are using bleach bottles, dip the metal caps into some kind of liquid rubber or paint after attaching them to the bottle. This prevents rusting.

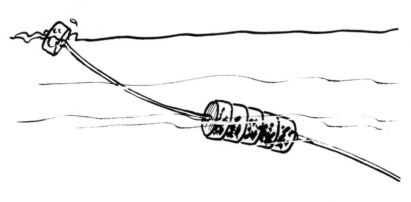

A safety float on the trap line provides visibility even in heavy tides or wind-whipped seas.

You can also add a safety float to your trapline by simply adding another float on a separate 10-foot line attached to your existing float. The smaller float will act as a marker to find the main line.

24

Floats and Boats

It is important to approach the trap against the wind and tide so you will not inadvertently drift over the float and get it caught in the propellor. If the wind and tide are in opposite directions, it is a good idea to make a test approach off to one side to see how the boat reacts, and then plan a proper, safe approach. As the boat gets close to the float, the engine should be put into neutral and the boat allowed to drift the last few feet to the trap. This is additional protection against getting the propellor fouled.

In a small boat, you can simply grab the float with your hand and pull in the trap. In a larger boat, use a gaff hook or boat hook and grasp the line at the trap end of the floats. If you twist the gaff, it will keep the line from slipping off. You can also put a ring at the top of your float line which makes it easier to grab.

When the trap reaches the gunwale, it is a good idea to pause for a minute to let it drain over the side before bringing it aboard. This also allows you to remove bits of seaweed and other debris.

HANDLING CRABS

After the trap is in the boat, you can simply turn it upside down and shake the crabs into the cockpit. You can also reach into the trap, but often the crabs will grab onto the netting or squeeze into a tight corner. If a crab grasps the trap mesh, it is better to just relax your grip and allow the crab to let go. Then you can grab him and jerk him out of the trap in one quick motion.

Crabs may be grasped by the rear legs and held upright to keep them from biting. They may also be grasped at the rear of the shell using thumb and fingers. The pointed legs will sometimes be able to poke at you, but the crab will not be able to get at you with his dangerous claws. Crabs have great strength in their claws and have been known to break a finger.

I have seen cans of clams which have been crushed into unrecognizable shape by hungry crabs, so use caution.

SORTING THE CATCH

Size limits vary in each area, as does the method of measurement. In B.C., the minimum size is 6½ inches across the widest part of the shell. In the U.S., some areas have a six-inch minimum width measured immediately in front of the widest point. While this is a somewhat narrower area, the 6½-inch measurement for B.C. is probably equivalent to the six-inch measurement in the U.S.

I find it convenient to have a measuring device so that I can quickly identify which crabs are legal. It consists simply of a piece

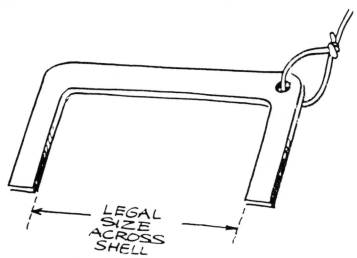

of plywood cut into a "C"-shaped caliper. If the crab is wider than the open space, it is a keeper.

All females, undersized crabs and "soft" crabs should be returned to the water unharmed. Female crabs can be easily identified by turning them on their backs. They have a wider spacing between the two rows of legs than do the males. Soft shelled crabs

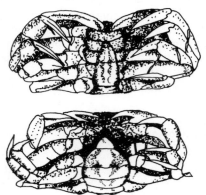

Underside of male (upper) and female dungeness crabs. Note the much broader and rounded gap between the legs of the female.

26

are those which have recently molted and the new shell has not yet filled out with meat. I return these crabs to the water very gently, but will keep those whose shells are partially hardened. The weight of the crab will also give you some indication of how it has filled out. This is a judgment call, and only experience will tell you how to choose crabs with sufficient meat.

An interesting phenomenon has developed in some areas where there is intense crabbing pressure. Some crabs never do get completely hard, and these crabs are returned to the water continually by commercial and sport crabbers. They have passed this tendency on to their offspring, and a whole new race of semi-soft crabs have developed in these areas. They are called "rubber legs" in the

APPROACH SLOWLY, DRIFTING AGAINST WIND/CURRENT...

mouth of the Columbia River. By keeping these semi-hardened crabs, we can prevent the population of rubber legs from increasing.

KEEPING THE CATCH FRESH

Crabs can live out of the water for long periods of time if their gill membranes are kept wet. They will die very quickly if left in the hot sun to dry out.

They can be stored in a wet burlap sack or a plastic garbage can or bucket. I sometimes even keep them in the fish box where they crawl under the catch to keep cool and moist. If I plan to keep crabs for some time before cleaning, I will place them in a large plastic garbage can filled with sea water which is changed every few hours during the heat of the day.

PROCESSING CRAB

When crab is purchased at a seafood counter, it is usually the whole crab, complete with entrails and bright red back and legs (the normally brownish shell turns red during cooking). In popular tourist areas such as Fisherman's Wharf in San Francisco, customers can watch the crab being thrown live into boiling water and cooked fresh right before their eyes. This traditional way of cooking crab allows the merchant to sell it at a lower price per pound, and also saves the labor of further cleaning, but there are some disadvantages.

A crab thrown into boiling water will tense its muscles as it scrambles frantically to escape. This can result in tougher meat. Cooking the entrails also changes the flavour in a way some find undesirable. I much prefer to kill the crabs and partially clean them before cooking. This has many advantages:

1. Only the meat and surrounding shell is cooked. This saves a great deal of space in the cooking pot. You can get up to three times as many crabs in the pot as compared to cooking them whole.

2. It cuts down some of the cooking odor and in my opinion improves the flavor.

3. It is easier to shell the meat because there are no entrails or slime attached to it.

4. I really believe the meat is more tender because the crab is killed instantly.

Cleaning Alternatives

There are several methods of killing the crab quickly and humanely:

1. Place a shovel or sharp-edged tool with the handle down in a large garbage can, with the shovel tip extending above the container. Grasp the crab by the legs with both hands, one hand for the right set of legs, and one for the left side. Hold the

crab above the edge of the shovel and pull down sharply, striking the underflap against the shovel. This should break the crab into three pieces. The underside will split down the middle, leaving two sections, each containing one set of legs and the attached body meat. The third section is the back and entrails, which will stick to the shovel or fall away into the garbage can.

A shovel placed upside down in a garbage pail makes a handy way to clean crabs.

2. Lay the crab on its back and use a knife or hatchet to split it down the middle. Simply lay the knife or hatchet along the flap and strike the back of the knife sharply with a mallet (or your fist) to break through the undershell but not through the carapace. Now grasp one set of legs and twist them away from the shell, bringing the attached body meat with them. Hold the

knife with the other hand to keep the crab shell in place. Then do the same for the other side.

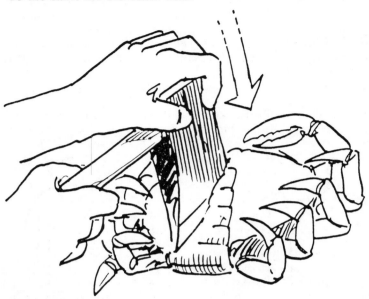

3. This method requires no special tools other than some protruding object such as the edge of a table, sharp rock or even the edge of a log. Grasp the crab by the legs and claws as

close as possible to the body. Pull them back so that the front edge of the shell is exposed. Now strike the front edge of the shell sharply against the protruding edge. This should be a sharp, swinging blow which will peel away the carapace and much of the crab entrails.

CRAB TALES

Crabs are the favorite food of the octopus. The giant Pacific octopus, which sometimes reach 100 pounds and more than 18 feet in total tentacle spread, can devour up to half a dozen large crabs per day.

I built a chain of tourist exhibits called Undersea Gardens, which were essentially large, submerged steel chambers surrounded by a fence to contain marine creatures in their natural habitat. The octopuses were the stars of our show, and we tried to keep them well fed with lots of fresh live crabs. We could always tell where the various octopuses were hiding by looking for the crab shells. In front of each den would be a neat little pile of complete crab shells with the shells picked clean of meat. The octopus kills the crab by biting it with its parrot-like beak and injecting a poison which tenderizes the meat to the extent that it can be sucked out, leaving the complete shell intact.

It was fascinating to watch an octopus capture a crab. As soon as the hungry octopus spotted the crab, he would turn a bright red color and move immediately over the crab like a giant spider. Grasping the crab with his tentacle suckers he would transfer it quickly to the centre of his body and paralyze it with one quick bite. Then he would tuck the crab under a tentacle and move off to hunt more prey.

We also had wolf eel dens in the Undersea Gardens and crab was also their favorite food. However, the crab shells outside the wolf eel den were mangled and crushed since the wolf eel eats the crab by crunching its shell, chewing the meat and discarding the crushed shell.

I had another interesting experience on a crabbing expedition with two elderly gentlemen as my guests. These gentlemen were from the U.S. mid-west and were fascinated by the whole crabbing procedure.

One trap was particularly heavy and I had a difficult time bringing it to the surface. I saw a huge octopus completely covering the top of the trap, evidently trying to get to the crabs inside. It looked like a beautiful specimen for the Undersea Gardens, so I called my guests to help me bring it on board. They took one look at the writhing eight-legged monster and retreated in horror to the cabin. I couldn't lift the trap on board, so I secured it to a cleat and grasped a tentacle as big around as my forearm and tried to pull the creature on board. I couldn't believe its strength and power as it hung on to the side of the trap, then pulled free and slithered back into the water.

My mid-western guests emerged from the cabin with a look of awe on their faces at a man who would do battle with an octopus! I'm sure they went home with a story which really wowed their home town friends.

Seals Steal Crab Bait

A most unusual problem has surfaced among crabbers along the Oregon coast. An explosion in the population of harbor seals has put sport crabbers in the position of trying to protect their bait from hungry seals!

One crabber wrote to me as follows:

I have been crabbing in a small estuary of the Salmon River about ten miles north of Lincoln City. We have seen many times when a crab ring seemingly does the impossible – goes up stream against the current! You guessed it – a seal was on the move with the ring in an attempt to get the bait.

I have also had friends who crab near Newport, Oregon. They report that the seals can even tear open a crab trap to get at the bait.

(Evidently the seals can even break into a stainless steel metal trap.)

To overcome this problem, many crabbers have started using chicken backs as bait. These chicken backs seem to attract crabs, with some crab rings catching as many as 15 or 20 specimens in a single set. Many of the crabs are small but the poultry baits seem quite successful.

Most important, according to my reports from Oregon, seals do not bother with the chicken flesh. To quote Douglas Raines:

I have witnessed this many times this past year – I will toss the ring in and right away I will see a seal nearby. He heads right for the float and down to the bottom, but never bothers the bait. Just today I had six seals working around the estuary. They checked the rings and went on their way without bothering the bait.

BEST BETS

TIME: In shallow water, high slack tide in late spring is best as crabs are in mating pairs and males are encumbered by females.

LOCATION: Sandy bottoms with good tidal action, off long sandy spits, off river mouths or in inside waters with sandy bottom and eel grass.

METHOD: Traps are best but crab rings also work well. Can be taken by hand in tidal pools at low tide; found under sand or seaweed. Use fresh bait. Clams and fish carcasses/entrails best.

CHAPTER II
SHRIMP
AND
PRAWNS

Shrimp and prawns have many similarities to crabs. They are both crustaceans; they have somewhat similar lifecycles; and are used in similar types of gourmet dishes. They are cousins of the delectable Maine lobster and the Longusta lobster of tropical waters. They are also related to the freshwater crayfish and the giant warm water prawns of the Bayou area in the Mississippi Delta. There are five varieties of shrimp in the north Pacific, all somewhat similar in appearance, but varying in size and habitat.

Adult shrimp breed in the fall and the female will carry the eggs on her abdomen during the winter. After the eggs hatch, the shrimp larvae drift about with planktonic organisms for about two months before dropping to the bottom. From this point on they tend to crawl on the bottom, although they can swim with rapid movements of their powerful tails.

All shrimp and prawns are males during the first two years, after which they make a remarkable transition and become females for the rest of their lives! This is one of nature's unique ways of ensuring survival. There are always plenty of young males to mate with the larger females.

The prawn is the largest of the north Pacific shrimp, reaching a length of nine inches over-all. It is found from Alaska to California and lives on rocky bottoms in 200 to 350 feet of water.

Side-striped shrimp are somewhat smaller and not nearly as plentiful. They reach up to eight inches and are found on a mud

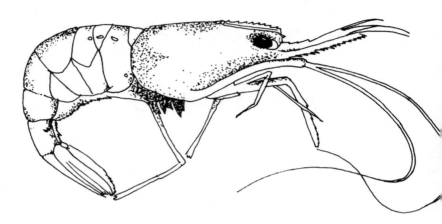

Prawns are the largest north Pacific shrimp reaching nine inches in length. The coon-striped shrimp (above) are smaller and most plentiful.

bottom in 250 to 350 feet of water. Their range is from Washington state to Alaska.

Next in size is the humpbacked shrimp which is five to six inches in length, and is found on mud bottoms in 100 to 300 feet of water from Washington to Alaska.

One of the most plentiful shrimp is the coon stripe which is found from California to Alaska and is about four or five inches long. It prefers a sand or gravel bottom with a good current. It is found in 100 to 300 feet of water during most of the year, but migrates into very shallow water in the evenings from August through November.

The smallest of the north Pacific shrimp is the pink shrimp which is only three or four inches in over-all length, and is found from Oregon to Alaska. It lives on mud bottoms in 60 to 350 feet of water.

Most sport fishing for shrimp and prawns is done with traps in very deep water, as indicated by the habitat information. The one exception is the coon stripe shrimp which supports a very popular fishery in shallow water, as described later in this section.

TRAP DESIGN

There are two basic types of shrimp traps. The most popular, especially for the person who builds his own, is simply a rectangular box with entrance tunnels at both ends. There are also rounded traps and pyramid-shaped traps with entrances in the top.

My own tests over a number of years have shown that the side entrance tunnel traps are more productive, just as side entrance tunnels catch more crabs. Shrimp are attracted to the trap primarily by the smell of the bait, and are more likely to enter a trap with an entrance tunnel leading directly off the bottom, rather than by the indirect route of crawling up the side of a trap to find the entrance.

Metal Framed Trap

A simple and effective prawn and shrimp trap can be constructed from a welded frame of ⅜-inch iron reinforcing bar with 12-inch ends and an over-all length of between 24 and 30 inches.

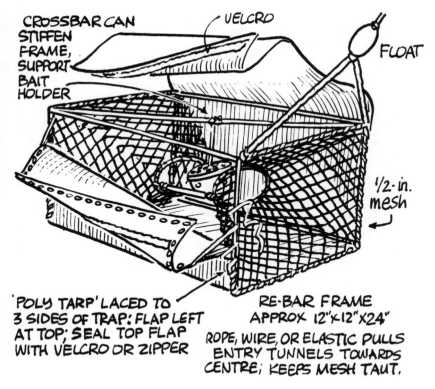

CROSSBAR CAN STIFFEN FRAME, SUPPORT BAIT HOLDER

VELCRO

FLOAT

½-in. mesh

'POLY TARP' LACED TO 3 SIDES OF TRAP: FLAP LEFT AT TOP; SEAL TOP FLAP WITH VELCRO OR ZIPPER

RE-BAR FRAME APPROX 12"×12"×24"

ROPE, WIRE, OR ELASTIC PULLS ENTRY TUNNELS TOWARDS CENTRE; KEEPS MESH TAUT.

35

Entrance cones slope in at an angle of about 45 degrees from both ends, with a 2½-inch ring at the inner end of each cone. This ring size is large enough to accommodate a large prawn, but will keep out most crabs, starfish, sculpins, and other undesirable predators.

One entrance tunnel should be hinged so that it can be swung open to empty the catch. Alternatively, a lid on the long axis of the trap can also be used for removal of the catch.

The Darker the Better

The trap frame should be covered with an opaque cloth or plastic material. Prawns and shrimp like a darkened area in which to feed and will enter a darkened area more readily than an open mesh trap which transmits light.

I had an interesting experience while testing various covering materials for my prawn traps. We were using a tightly woven plastic swimming pool cover material on our traps and measured the number of prawns per trap.

We then added a second layer of plastic over half of the traps which cut light transmission drastically. We were amazed to find that our catch in the darkened traps was almost twice as great as in the traps with only a single covering.

This discovery was especially dramatic because we were using traps which had previously been fished with a single covering, and these same traps now caught almost twice as many prawns. The only difference between the two sets of traps was the second layer of covering material.

Since the first edition of this book went to press, we have continued our experiments and have changed our thinking somewhat. While the darkened traps produce the most prawns, they do have a lot of resistance when pulling. Our latest tests have found that open meshed traps produce almost as many prawns as the covered ones and are much easier to handle.

In my earlier book, *How to Catch Shellfish*, I showed a prawn trap which was used in fisheries department tests and had good catches. This trap was made from unpainted plywood with entrance tunnels at both ends. This device worked well, but the buoyant plywood made it necessary to add heavy rocks or iron bars to hold the trap safely on the bottom. This resulted in a very heavy and unwieldy trap. In my opinion a metal frame covered with plastic is a much more efficient and effective design.

BAITING THE TRAP

Shrimp and prawns are somewhat similar to crabs in their bait preferences. They much prefer fresh bait to tainted or spoiled meat. I have used clams, fish heads, fish entrails, fish blood and even canned cat food as prawn bait.

Commercial shrimp and prawn operators use chunks of meat from dogfish sharks and fresh herring as their favorite baits. Both of these baits give off a strong oily odor in the water, and are also somewhat tough and keep well in a trap over several days.

FOLDING PRAWN TRAP

'POLY TARP' IS SEWN TO TUNNEL MESH;
NOT ATTACHED TO FRAME

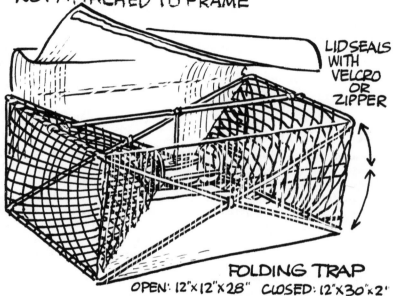

LID SEALS WITH VELCRO OR ZIPPER

FOLDING TRAP
OPEN: 12"x 12"x 28"   CLOSED: 12"x 30"x 2"

'POLY TARP SIDES & 'LID', JOINED TO MESH
END TUNNELS, FORM 'CAGE'. WHEN
METAL 'X' FRAME IS OPENED AND HELD
BY TENSION OF BAIT HOLDER ELASTIC, PRAWN
TRAP IS READY TO USE.

RELEASE ELASTIC AND FOLD FRAME
FLAT INSIDE LOOSE 'CAGE' FOR TRANS-
PORT, STORAGE.

I have found that these two baits are the most effective for prawns and shrimp. I find herring baits best for short sets (under 24 hours) and dogfish more effective for longer trap sets.

Placing bait in plastic jars or cups with holes punched in the sides helps preserve the bait for longer periods of time. The smell continues to attract the shrimp, but they cannot get at it once they are in the trap. If the bait are also frozen, it further extends the time that odors will be released into the water as the bait inside the jars thaws and gradually releases oil and bits of meat into the surrounding water.

A large quantity of bait is also helpful in improving shrimp and prawn catches. I will often include one or two bait jars in the trap and add several fish heads, whole herring threaded on a piece of stainless wire, or some frozen fish carcasses to provide a large quantity of bait inside the trap.

As with crab traps, it is important that the bait be tied, wrapped, or wired firmly in the trap in the area between the entrance tunnels. Otherwise the bait will drift to the corners of the trap at the base of the entrance tunnels and the shrimp or prawns will feed on it from the outside of the trap.

TRAP LOCATION

Good locations for prawns and shrimp can be found by studying marine charts, and looking for the proper type of bottom as outlined in the description of habitat for each shrimp species.

I prefer to fish for prawns, the largest and, in my opinion, the tastiest of the north Pacific shrimp species. These are usually found on a rocky bottom in a long narrow inlet. Since they inhabit rocky crevices and caves along shelving shorelines, it is important to set the trap carefully at the proper depth, usually between 250 and 350 feet.

It is best to avoid areas with a strong tidal current, since the pressure on this long length of line can easily dislodge the trap and let it drop into deeper water. This will either submerge the float or, if the float is more buoyant than the trap weight, the whole rig will float away with the tide.

TRAP LINE

Use at least 300 feet of polypropylene or similar plastic line of about 3/16-inch diameter. These plastic ropes are light and will not absorb water. They have far more strength than you need, but this thickness will not cut into your hand as badly as a thinner line. Do not use nylon line since it is far more expensive and its stretch is a significant drawback. Heavier lines are not desirable because they create a lot of drag in heavy current and could result in the trap being dragged into deeper water by strong tidal action.

Bleach bottles can be used as floats, but be sure to get ones with plastic lids and seal them with silicon to prevent leakage. A better bet is to buy small plastic or cork floats from a fisheries supply store and string four or five of them on the end of the line.

The best type of float has a pole and flag attached for easy pickup of the trap. Prawn traps set in deep water offshore can be almost impossible to find if the water is even slightly choppy. It is also advisable to take gunsight marks in two directions to help you locate the trap. (See page 87.)

PULLING THE TRAP

I have fished prawns and shrimp from boats ranging from a six-foot dinghy to a 60-foot yacht. Pulling a trap from approximately 300 feet of water (the length of a football field!) is quite a chore. It will give you a lot of good exercise and is great for the pectorals.

A pulley on the edge of the gunwale and a steady rhythm make pulling traps easier.

I find it easiest to lead the line over the gunwale and pull horizontally, allowing me to use my back as well as my arms. Leaning over the side of the boat and pulling with arms only is extremely tiring and hard on the back.

Attaching a small pulley to the edge of a gunwale or a davit through which to string the trap line is extremely helpful in reducing friction when pulling the trap. You can also use a smooth-edged gunwale (stainless steel or aluminum rail) to help ease the line friction.

Most of my prawning experiments have been conducted out of a small dinghy and I worked out a very effective method of pulling traps. Using an oarlock or a small pulley to guide the line, I heave back with my whole body and haul in the line in meter-long pulls.

The rocking action of the boat during this pulling action further increases its effectiveness. As you haul back, the boat will roll with your weight shift, raising the gunwale over which the line is pulling. As you lean forward to take another grip on the line, the gunwale drops back. This creates a momentary slack line which can add at least a foot to the next heaving motion, resulting in a four-foot total pull. This rocking, pulling action develops into a smooth rhythm, almost like rowing a boat.

It is important to keep this rhythm to maintain the upward momentum of the trap. When you stop to rest (and I often do, especially when pulling the second trap!) the upward momentum stops, and it takes extra effort to overcome the inertia and start the trap moving again.

SEVERAL TRAPS ON ONE LINE

Commercial shrimp operators set many traps on one line, often stretching for hundreds of yards across the shrimping grounds. These traps are pulled with power gurdies and emptied and re-baited in one continuous production line setup.

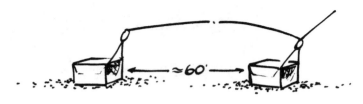

Several traps can be strung on one line but it is best to keep to a maximum of two traps on any one line; otherwise the weight is too much to lift by hand.

Sport fishing for prawns can also be done with two or more traps, but they become very heavy to lift by hand. Two traps per line is the practical maximum in my opinion.

Adding a second trap is simple. Attach a second trap with approximately 60 feet of line to a normal single trap setup. This will give proper spacing between traps. However, you must be careful to keep moving at the time the traps are set or they will end up too close together and both traps will attract prawns or shrimp from the same area, cutting down on the catch per trap. Spreading the traps allows the drawing of prawns or shrimp from a larger over-all area.

CATCHING COON STRIPE SHRIMP

Coon stripe shrimp move into shallow water in late August and can be caught well into November. The shrimp move in after dark, with peak catches sometimes coming after midnight.

Most coon stripe are caught with very simple nets. A metal hoop such as a bicycle wheel is covered with small mesh netting, burlap, or window screening material, so that it forms a very shallow basket. The bait (fish head, fish carcass, can of catfood or sardines) is tied to the centre of the net ring and lowered to the bottom in 10 to 30 feet of water. Docks, piers, marinas, breakwater walls and other similar spots are good locations for this shallow water shrimp operation.

Traps are baited and set at dusk and pulled every five to 30 minutes depending on the quantity of shrimp moving inshore. Normally the shrimp move in small groups and 15- to 30-minute intervals are sufficient for emptying the trap.

However, sometimes the shrimp come in great waves, overrunning the trap in a few minutes. These are the exciting times when gleeful shrimpers pull their traps every five minutes and empty a good load of tasty crustaceans.

This type of shrimping is a very pleasant family outing. Small bonfires are built on the beach, and groups of friends and neighbors toast marshmallows and sip hot beverages while catching and cooking their seafood harvest.

It is also possible to catch coon stripe shrimp along any protected shoreline with a flashlight and small kitchen sieve. Wearing some waterproof boots, the shrimper simply walks quietly along the shore shining the flashlight at the water's edge. The shrimp eyes glow brightly in the glare of the flashlight, so they can be easily spotted and scooped up with the sieve.

COOKING SHRIMP AND PRAWNS

Shrimp and prawns are cooked in a manner similar to crabs, except the cooking time is much shorter. Shrimp and prawns should be kept in a bucket of cold sea water as soon as they are caught, and cooked as soon as is practical. Drain the water and pour the live shrimp into boiling salt water. Two or three minutes is sufficient time for smaller shrimp, and five minutes maximum for large prawns. They are cooked when they turn pink. It's better to undercook the prawns. A slightly undercooked prawn is much better than an overcooked one.

I prefer to clean my shrimp before cooking just as I do with crabs. Simply grasp the prawn or shrimp by the tail near the mid-section and twist off the head and legs with one quick motion. This cuts in half the volume to be cooked, and you can get up to 50 good-sized prawns in a saucepan.

After the shrimp are cooked, peel the shell from the meat or peel the front section of shell and pull the meat free while pinching the tail between thumb and forefinger.

With larger prawns, you may wish to pull out the thin "vein" that runs up the centre of the meat. Unless this vein is quite dark in color, I don't usually bother since it doesn't seem to affect the taste.

SHRIMP RECIPES

Shrimp and prawns (as well as crabs) can be prepared in many tasty dishes. *How to Cook Your Catch*, by Jean Challenger, contains many simple recipes which can be prepared on board a boat or at a campsite.

BEST BETS

PLACE: Long narrow inlets. Use charts to locate areas with rocky bottoms along shelving shorelines.

LOCATION: Prawns: Rock bottom in 250-350 feet of water.
   Coon strip shrimp: Late August through November, evenings in shallow water.

METHOD: Prawns: Enclosed (not mesh) side entrance traps. Use fresh bait; clams, fish heads/entrails, chunks dogfish best bait. Frozen bait also works well.

PREPARATION/COOKING: Store in cold sea water, cook as soon as practical. Best cooked live in boiling water for two to three minutes (five minutes if large).

CHAPTER III
OYSTERS

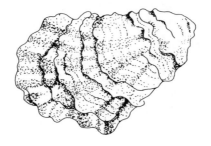

Pacific or Japanese oysters can be found from B.C. to California. They were originally imported from Japan in the form of "spat," the name given oysters in the larval stage. Spat is gathered by placing old oyster shells in an area where live oysters are spawning. The tiny larvae attach themselves to the smooth side of the old oyster shell and begin to grow. There is a large industry in Japan, collecting spat and shipping the spat-laden shells to commercial oyster growers in B.C., California, Oregon and Washington.

In recent years, more and more of the spat is grown locally. Many oyster leases are in areas with water warm enough for natural spawning and imported spat is no longer necessary.

Oysters spawn in August and the newly hatched larvae require warm water temperatures for 10 days to two weeks in order to survive. Most oyster leases are in protected bays and inlets where water temperatures frequently exceed 70 degrees Fahrenheit at the surface during the warm summer months.

After the oyster spawns in August, the meat is thin and watery and the oysters are not very tasty. The oyster produces a white starchy substance called glycogen and gradually becomes fatter. It lies dormant through the cold winter months and is normally excellent eating at this time. In March or April oysters may produce more glycogen as the water temperatures begin to rise slightly. In my opinion, oysters are at their absolute peak in March, April and early May as glycogen levels reach their annual peak.

By late May or early June, the body chemistry begins to change dramatically. A large portion of the oyster's glycogen is transformed into reproductive material, either eggs or sperm. Oysters can be either male or female and some oysters change sex from one year to the next. Obviously it is important to the oyster whether it

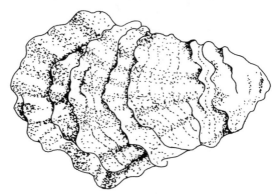

Originally imported from Japan, the Pacific oyster is now found from B.C. to California and are at their best in March, April and early May.

is male or female, but it makes no difference for eating. As the chemical composition of the oyster changes in June and into July, the flavor of the meat deteriorates considerably. It has a much stronger taste with a distinct iodine flavor which many people find objectionable. These changes continue until they spawn in August.

Barbecued oysters

Most oysters are gathered by recreational boaters during the warm summer months when they are in their least palatable condition. However, barbecuing oysters in the shell seems to mask a great deal of the "pre-spawning" flavor and barbecued oysters with a bit of sauce are often quite tasty.

Cooking oysters on a barbecue is very simple, and saves the problem of opening the shell. Place the oyster over a hot fire with the rounded shell down and cook until the oyster relaxes its muscle and shows a slight gap between the shells.

Remove the oyster with a pair of tongs or a heavy glove and pry open the shell with a knife or fork. Then eat the oyster with a little barbecue sauce or a combination of ketchup and lemon juice. MMMMMmmmmmmmm!

44

PICKING OYSTERS

Commercial oysters are usually raised from spat planted on their leased beds, but in warm water areas (where oysters spawn naturally) the spat will spread well beyond oyster leases and settle into nearby warm water bays and inlets.

After about three weeks in the free swimming larval stage, the young oyster will attach itself to a clean, hard object. It uses a potent glue near the hinge to attach itself to this spot for the rest of its life. If it has attached itself to a small stone or other movable object, it may drift with the tide, but otherwise remains fixed.

Where to Find Oysters

The most likely place to find oysters, therefore, is in quiet bays and backwaters with warm temperatures.

The oysters will be found almost entirely between the high and low tide marks, since only the surface waters are warm enough. Some oysters are washed into deeper water and may survive there, but they are more likely to be eaten by starfish or other predators.

In areas where oysters are plentiful, they will be standing on their edges with only the hinge end attached to the rock. These are simple to break off with a quick gentle blow from a wooden stick, screwdriver, or even your foot.

Some oysters are glued flat to rocky surfaces and are very difficult to remove. They can be pried off with a heavy knife or even a chisel.

SHUCKING OYSTERS

This is a very simple task when you know the location of the adductor muscles which hold the shells tightly closed. Insert a knife between the shells and cut the adductor muscle and the shell will pop open easily.

Inserting the knife between the tightly closed shells can be difficult, but becomes easier with practice. Some people break away a bit of shell at the outer lips of the oyster to expose a more obvious crack between the upper and lower shell.

OYSTER SIZE

Oyster growth is dependent on how much time it spends underwater. Oysters pump water continuously through their food filters and will grow 24 hours a day if completely submerged. Oysters nearest the low tide mark therefore grow faster than those higher on the beach.

Commercial oyster growers often hang the oysters on strings below floating rafts to get maximum growth and easy harvesting. Warm water temperatures also speed oyster growth.

Some oysters are ready for harvest in about a year, but others, in colder water, take two years or more to reach edible size. When the oyster is between two and three inches long, it is ideal for eating raw on the half shell. Four-inch oysters are good for frying, broiling or in oyster stews. Oysters over five inches long are okay when chopped up and fried or used in oyster stew, but the smaller ones are better for all uses, in my opinion.

Some Pacific oysters grow absolutely huge. Specimens up to 11 inches in length with a weight of 2½ pounds have been recorded by biologists. These oysters are as tender as ever, but the digestive glands are very large, and the stomach may be full of oily planktonic organisms, making them less palatable.

RAW OYSTERS

My father and mother used to eat raw oysters as a gourmet delicacy. My brother and I watched with a mixture of awe and revulsion as our parents ate the slimy-looking things.

"You've got to chew them," my father would say. "If you swallow them whole, it's a complete waste."

After I got up the courage to eat raw oysters myself, I found that my father's advice was absolutely correct. If you swallow an oyster whole, the experience is as bad as you imagined it. There is no taste, only a cold, slimy mass sliding down your throat. When you chew the oyster, only then is the delicate flavor released.

Keeping live oysters

Oysters will live for many months if stored in a bucket or barrel and covered with a burlap sack dampened with sea water. The barrel should have a drain in the bottom to remove accumulated water, or a wire mesh to hold oysters above the water collecting in the bottom of the barrel. The burlap sack should be moistened with sea water every day or so.

Another good method is to suspend the oysters in an open mesh plastic basket, perhaps hanging from a wharf or dock. This keeps the oysters above the bottom and away from starfish and other predators.

COMMERCIAL OYSTER LEASES

Some oyster leases are in well-defined areas with clear boundary markers. However, many others are not marked at all and it is difficult for a boater or outdoorsman to know whether he is harvesting wild or cultivated oysters.

Sometimes you can see a pile of oyster shells and a shucking house nearby as an indication of commercial activity, but other leases are far from the place of processing. I know one oyster lease off a small island near Chemainus with no markers whatsoever. The commercial grower brings in a large barge every few days and harvests the oysters to take back to the processing plant.

OYSTER REGULATIONS

Oyster gathering is controlled in each province and state some-

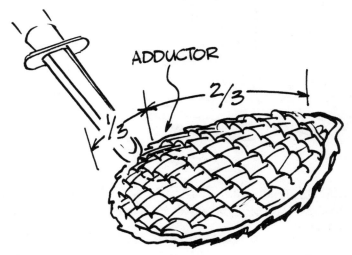

Shucking oysters is simple once the adductor muscles are located.

what differently, but the intent is to maintain a sustained yield of oysters.

B.C. currently (1988) allows 15 oysters a person, or one-half litre of shucked oysters a day, with a two-day possession limit.

Washington state allows 18 oysters which must be shucked before removal from the beach and the shells replaced approximately where the oysters were taken. This is to ensure that future oyster spat has the old smooth oyster shell surface on which to anchor.

NATIVE WILD OYSTERS

Many years ago there was a plentiful supply of native or Olympia oysters in Puget Sound and the coastal waters of B.C.

DON'T BOTHER TRYING TO CUT OYSTER'S HINGE -- A WASTE OF TIME!

PLACE OYSTER, ROUNDED SIDE DOWN, ON A FIRM SURFACE, HINGE TOWARD YOU. HOLD IN PLACE AS SHOWN.

INSERT TIP OF KNIFE BETWEEN SHELLS NEAR ADDUCTOR. BREAK OFF A BIT OF SHELL IF NEEDED. TWIST AND PUSH THE BLADE BETWEEN THE SHELLS. SUCKING NOISE AND WATER DRAINING OUT MEANS SUCTION HOLDING SHELLS TOGETHER HAS BROKEN.

ONCE BLADE IS INSIDE, LEVER HANDLE UPWARD AND PUSH POINT DOWN, TO SEVER BOTTOM ADD-UCTOR MUSCLE.

REMOVE TOP SHELL AND FREE THE MEAT BY CUTTING TOP ADDUCTOR.

SCOOP MEAT FROM BOTTOM SHELL

Native oyster spat needs a hard smooth surface on which to anchor. Intensive harvesting pressure removed most of the old shells, which reduced new habitat possibilities. Olympia oysters also smother easily in mud or silt.

There are still Olympia oysters available, but they are difficult to distinguish from the Pacific or Japanese variety. The edges of the shell are more scalloped and the shell is thin and more delicate. They tend to be glued flat against smooth rocks or attached to the underside of large boulders where they are difficult to remove. Since they seldom exceed 1½ inches in length, they are not of much interest to most oyster harvesters looking for the larger Pacific oyster.

PEARL OYSTERS

The edible oysters contain some pearls, but they are just blobs of calcium with no commercial value. They are very dull and cannot be properly polished.

Pearl oysters are a completely different variety (not considered edible) which have a more lustrous mother-of-pearl shell to produce the commercial pearls.

MUSSELS

Mussels are related to oysters and, like oysters, are relatively easy to find. There are two different mussels found in the north Pacific — the blue mussel or bay mussel and the California mussel.

Blue mussels

The blue mussel is the gourmet delicacy found on menus in fine restaurants in Europe and, to a lesser extent, in North America. It

The blue mussel is found in quiet water all along the B.C. coast and is considered a delicacy by many.

is widely distributed along the coast and is very adaptable to a wide variety of conditions. It can survive very warm water temperatures and low salinity; occurs in large numbers almost anywhere there is quiet water and is often found clinging to rocks, floats, pilings, logs and anything which will allow it to filter large quantities of planktonic organisms. An ideal habitat is the underside of floating docks where the mussels can be submerged (and feeding) 24 hours a day.

Blue mussels seldom attain a length over two inches, and most are a lot smaller due to crowding together in large clusters. They are especially susceptible to pollution since they pick up toxic materials quite easily. Even a few boats can contaminate nearby mussels with petroleum waste as well as sewage refuse.

Blue mussels have a cream colored meat, but some have a light orange cast.

California mussels

This is a very large mussel indeed. It can grow to a length of 10

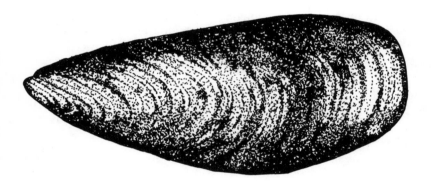

The California mussel is a very large mussel found primarily on the open coast. Look for it on rocks near open surf.

inches and is found primarily on the open coast-line where salinity is high. It is often found attached to rocks adjacent to the open surf.

The shell is thin with a black covering which peels when dried out. The meat is reddish or bright orange.

Horse mussels

This is not a mussel at all, but a member of the clam family. It grows to eight inches in length, is wedge shaped and rounded at both ends. The outside of the shell has a thin, shiny brown covering. It lives individually on bits of gravel or sand.

Cooking mussels

After you are certain that the mussels are taken from unpolluted waters and there is no "red tide" in the area, store the mussels out of water but covered with damp seaweed or a burlap sack. They should be washed under fresh running water and scrubbed with a strong brush to remove algae and other debris.

Fill the bottom of a pot or electric frypan with a shallow layer of water, add the mussels, and cover with a loose lid.

Mussels should be steamed approximately 20 minutes until the

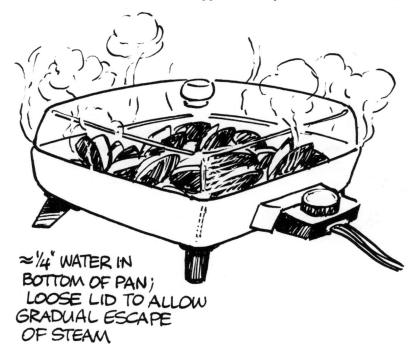

≈¼" WATER IN
BOTTOM OF PAN;
LOOSE LID TO ALLOW
GRADUAL ESCAPE
OF STEAM

shells have opened. You should discard any mussels which don't have tightly closed shells before cooking.

Mussels and little neck clams can be steamed in the same pan. They go well together served with melted butter. Mussels can also be used as a major ingredient in bouillabaisse or they can be sautéed or even deep fried.

Mussels have the same seasonal pattern as oysters. They are soft and contain reproductive material in the summer months, and tend to be thin and watery after spawning.

"R" MONTH

There is a popular misconception that oysters should only be eaten when there is an "R" in the month. Months without "R" are the warm summer months of May through August. These are the months when oysters can most easily spoil. In the days before proper refrigeration, I'm sure many people became ill from eating contaminated seafood in warmer weather.

A more important factor is that the summer months are the likely time for outbreaks of "red tide" or paralytic shellfish poisoning. These outbreaks normally appear between April and November with the highest concentrations in the non-"R" months of May through August.

BEST BETS

TIME: Taste best in winter, March, April and early May when glycogen levels high.

LOCATION: Between high and low tide marks in quiet bays and backwaters.

METHOD: Break off rocks with hand, foot, stick or suitable tool.

PREPARATION/COOKING: Break away edges of shell to insert knife and cut adductor muscles. Can be eaten raw, steamed, barbecued or in chowders and stews.

CHAPTER IV
CLAMS
AND
CLAMMING

Unlike oysters and mussels, which can be found fully exposed and right out in the open for gathering, clams are buried in the sand or mud. Some knowledge of their habitat is important to find them. Clams are bivalves and members of the mollusk family.

With the exception of the razor clam, which is found on sandy beaches exposed to the open coast, all clams are found in the protected waters of bays and inlets. While oysters and mussels filter sea water as it passes by the rock or pier to which they are attached, clams need to suck the water through a siphon extending to the surface from their home under the surface.

The water passes through the gills where food particles, mostly plankton, are filtered out. The filtered sea water is returned through a second tube in the siphon and expelled.

Clams propagate by expelling sperm into the water where fertilization takes place. The eggs divide and develop into swimming larvae. After about three weeks of feeding on plankton, the larvae settle to the bottom in the intertidal zone and crawl on their already well developed "feet." They attach themselves to something firm during which important changes take place in their bodies.

After reaching about ¼ of an inch in length, they burrow into the sand or gravel where they remain for the rest of their lives. They are capable of only small vertical movements from now on.

Many larvae are carried to unsuitable areas and die. However, larvae are produced in prolific numbers and are carried to new areas which helps spread the clam population. Larvae may move as much as 50 miles from the original spawning area.

Butter clams are one of several varieties found on the B.C. coast; they have been known to live as long as 20 years.

Clams grow from feeding on plankton during the time when their siphons are covered with water. Since there is more abundant plankton during the summer months, clams grow much faster when the water temperatures are highest. The growth rings on the outer shell of a clam are a result of the seasonal changes in growth rate. The age of a clam can be measured in a similar manner to reading the growth rings on a tree. Sometimes there are false rings caused by interrupted summer growth, but the basic annual growth rings are usually more pronounced. Growth slows with age, so rings are closer toward the outer edge of the shell.

Clams can live to a surprising age. Butter clams have been known to survive more than 20 years. The types of clams covered in this book are distributed from the Queen Charlotte Islands to the California coast. The most important are the little neck, butter clam, cockle, horse clam or gaper, and the soft shell clam.

HARVESTING CLAMS

Generally speaking, the smaller clams are found close to the surface, and the larger clams are deeper, sometimes as much as 18 inches under the surface. These depth differentials are due primarily to the length of the siphon. Smaller clams have shorter siphons and have to be nearer the surface, while the larger clams can reach further up to the surface and live at greater depths.

Larger clams are usually found lower in the intertidal zone and are exposed only during the lowest tides. The only major exception is the soft shell clam which is often buried more than a foot under the surface, yet is found quite high on the beach.

Digging equipment

I use a small garden spade or shovel for digging clams, but the traditional tool for most clams is a long handled four-tined fork usually called a potato fork. Another convenient tool is a hoe-like garden rake with tines from four to six inches in length.

The fork or shovel should be inserted the full depth of the tool and the sand and gravel turned over next to the hole. Pick through the pile to find buried clams, or rake it with your fork. I am very careful to examine the sand or gravel, squeezing all lumps and rinsing rocks to uncover hidden clams.

It is a good idea to dig in a straight line. If you dig in one spot and pile up one large mound of sand and gravel, the small clams buried under the mound will not survive. This is just not good conservation, and destroys the future harvest. Straight line digging also allows you to cover the available beach in a more systematic manner.

The larger and deeper clams will probably require a shovel to remove the overburden. Digging for the very deep gapers (horse clams) requires a heavy duty spade and lots of muscle power.

CLEANING CLAMS

Clams should be soaked in cold salt water for four to eight hours. Do not use fresh water. It will kill clams. The soaking time allows them to spit out the grit and sand in their bodies.

Some people add a bit of oatmeal or cornmeal to the water in which the clams are soaked. The clam keeps feeding and will suck in this oatmeal and you will end up with a stuffed clam!

Soft shell clams, large butter clams and horse clams are cleaned as follows:

1. Cut the shell away from the flesh and remove the black portions and the green worm-like glands.

2. Rinse the remaining parts in running water.

3. The necks should be skinned with a sharp knife and the two tubes of the neck should be cut so they can be flattened for frying. Butter clams especially can store toxins in the black tip of the neck, so it is a good idea to cut this off prior to cooking.

BUTTER CLAM

1. OPEN CLAM: SLIDE KNIFE BETWEEN SHELLS, SEVER BOTH ADDUCTORS.

2. REMOVE BODY FROM SHELLS; CUT OR PULL MANTLE MUSCLES OFF BODY AT EACH END NEAR ADDUCTOR MUSCLES.

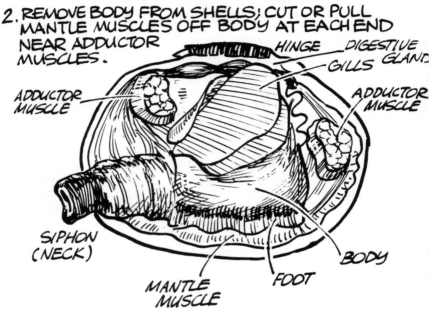

HINGE   DIGESTIVE GLAND.
GILLS
ADDUCTOR MUSCLE
ADDUCTOR MUSCLE
SIPHON (NECK)
MANTLE MUSCLE
FOOT
BODY

3. REMOVE & SAVE ADDUCTOR MUSCLES.

4. STRIP OFF AND DISCARD THE SIPHON AND GILLS.

5. REMOVE AND DISCARD THE DARK DIGESTIVE GLAND FROM TOP OF BODY.

PREPARING CLAMS

Large clams have tough, fibrous necks. In fact, the larger the clam, the tougher the neck. If they are too tough for frying, they can be ground up to make clam chowder or deep fried clam fritters.

56

(They also would make good bait for sole and flounder. See the section on bottom fish.)

The little neck clam and Manila clam are often called butter clam in error because the popular way to eat them is dipped in melted butter. This traditional way of cooking is very simple. Put about ¼ inch of water in a frying pan or any shallow pan and steam the clams under a loose fitting cover until they pop open. This usually

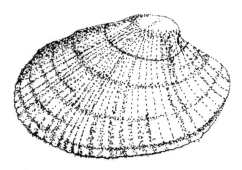

Often mistaken for a butter clam, the little neck clam is best eaten steamed.

takes 15 to 20 minutes. Then just dip them in melted butter and eat them right out of the shell.

EATING TOUGH AND TENDER CLAMS

The distinctive flavor of clams makes all of them tasty eating, but some are more tender than others. Little necks, Manilas and soft shell clams are the most tender, and can be eaten right from the shell. Small butter clams are tender, but toughen as they grow larger.

The tougher clams include the cockles, gapers and the larger butter clams. However, there are many ways to enjoy these clams. The adductor muscles from large cockles can be fried in a manner similar to scallops. Horse clams have most of their edible meat in the neck which is covered with a tough skin. The skin can be removed after scalding in boiling water, leaving a delicious white meat. It may be still somewhat tough, but can be minced for easier chewing.

All clams are excellent in chowder, but the cockles, gapers and large butter clams should be chopped up before adding to the broth.

Clams are at their best during the winter months, but the change from winter to summer is far less drastic than for oysters.

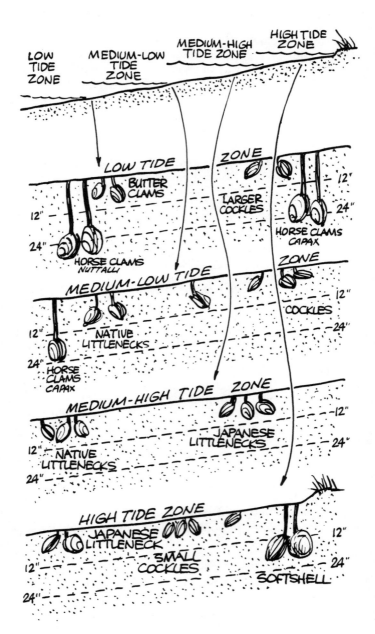

LOW TIDE ZONE
MEDIUM-LOW TIDE ZONE
MEDIUM-HIGH TIDE ZONE
HIGH TIDE ZONE

LOW TIDE ___ ZONE
BUTTER CLAMS
LARGER COCKLES
12"
24"
HORSE CLAMS CAPAX
12"
24"
HORSE CLAMS NUTTALLI

MEDIUM-LOW TIDE ___ ZONE
12"
COCKLES
24"
NATIVE LITTLENECKS
12"
24"
HORSE CLAMS CAPAX

MEDIUM-HIGH TIDE ZONE
12"
JAPANESE LITTLENECKS
24"
12" NATIVE LITTLENECKS
24"

HIGH TIDE ZONE
JAPANESE LITTLENECK
12"
SMALL COCKLES
24"
SOFTSHELL
12"
24"

STORING LIVE CLAMS

Clams are more difficult to keep alive for long periods than oysters. Placed in a small bucket, clams will deplete the oxygen and suffocate. This situation can be alleviated somewhat by stirring and splashing the water, but this only helps for a short time.

Clams will keep dry and cool for several days in a refrigerator or even a well insulated picnic cooler. Be careful that water draining from the clams does not collect in the bottom and suffocate those at the bottom of the container. Using a wire mesh to hold the clams off the bottom is a good idea in this instance.

Clams can also be put on a bed of seaweed and covered with a sack moistened with sea water (or even more seaweed). If you are camping on the beach, clams can be placed in a burlap or other porous sack and anchored to the beach with a rope. The tide will come in over the clams and keep them alive and healthy. Leave plenty of room in the sack so water can circulate freely.

If you are living on a boat, the clams can be hung in a sack over the side. However, this often results in clams packed tight in the bottom of the sack and in danger of suffocation.

Little necks are easiest to keep, and horse clams most difficult because their gaping shell allows them to dry out rapidly. Butter clams have a weaker adductor muscle and are used to the pressure of the surrounding sand to keep their shells closed. If you plan to keep butter clams longer than overnight, it might be a good idea to wrap a rubber band around each one.

RAZOR CLAMS

Razor clams are distributed widely in most areas where there are wide stretches of surf-pounded sand. They are not found in B.C.

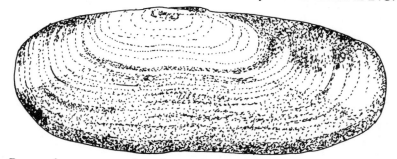

Razor clams are not found in inside waters. Look for them in surf-pounded sand.

interior waters or Puget Sound, but are plentiful along the open beaches of B.C., Washington, Oregon and Northern California.

The heaviest concentrations are found on the lower edges of the beaches where they are covered with water most of the time.

Most razor clam digging is done at the lowest possible tides in the sand near the water's edge. You can get clams in the water itself if you have a sharp eye to see the end of the siphon.

Not only are razor clams found in a completely different environment from the bay clams, they are also far more active. While the bay clams are extremely passive and seldom move in their entire lives, the razor clam is a real "athlete"!

In fact, a razor clam can dig into the sand faster than you can dig with your shovel, as you will soon find out when you pursue them. When the sand is wet, the razor clam can dig as fast as nine inches per minute. It accomplishes this feat with the aid of a large, muscular foot.

The foot is extended into the sand where it spreads out to form an effective anchor. It uses other muscles to pull itself downward against this anchor point. The razor clam has a thin, streamlined, elongated shell with a smooth surface which aids in these rapid movements.

However, the clam's movements are mostly vertical. It seldom moves horizontally. Fisheries departments have done tests on

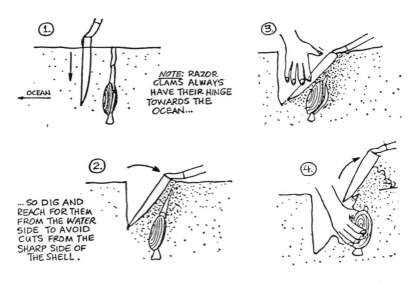

① OCEAN

NOTE: RAZOR CLAMS ALWAYS HAVE THEIR HINGE TOWARDS THE OCEAN...

② ...SO DIG AND REACH FOR THEM FROM THE WATER SIDE TO AVOID CUTS FROM THE SHARP SIDE OF THE SHELL.

③

④

razor clams and found that they stay in essentially the same location throughout their lives.

Most razor clams are dug in the hour before and the hour after the lowest tides of the year. Digging is also more productive if the water is calm. (No high surf continually covering the digging area.)

Nighttime low tides in the winter are also good for harvesting razor clams, but the clam "shows" are harder to spot by artificial light at night.

EQUIPMENT

You will need a good set of rubber boots and raingear to keep yourself comfortable in the turbulent area at the edge of the surf.

For digging the clams, a narrow bladed shovel (sometimes called a "clam gun") allows the digger to get down to the clam without having to lift a heavy load of sand. Regular garden shovels can be used, but you will have to expend far more effort per clam.

FINDING THE CLAM "SHOW"

Walking along the water's edge, look for the clam to squirt or look for a small dimple (about the size of the head of a pencil) where he has withdrawn his neck. If you jump on the sand or thump it with the back of your shovel it will often disturb the clam and cause him to reveal his location. In the water itself you can often see a little bit of the neck sticking above the water as the surf recedes. (Look for a V-shaped ripple in the receding water.)

CATCHING THE SPEEDSTER

No single procedure can be established as the correct method for digging razor clams. Several slightly different methods are used by the commercial diggers and experienced sportsmen, all of which seem to produce satisfactory results.

The method most commonly used is to put the shovel quite close to the clam "show" (indentation in the sand) on the ocean side and push the blade down vertically or slightly toward the clam. The shovel handle is then pushed horizontally to compress the sand around the clam.

SAND TRAPS CLAM

This tightly packed sand keeps the clam from using its foot to move rapidly down into the sand. The hand is then placed in behind the shovel in the space made when the sand was compressed. The shovel is removed quickly and the clam is seized before it has a chance to start its downward movement.

Another procedure used is to scoop out a shovelful of sand beside the clam show and reach in. This technique is used with great success by some commercial diggers, but it takes very fast action and nimble fingers to make it work.

These methods work only in wet sand when the clam is feeding at the surface or just below it. Working in dry sand is referred to as a "mining operation" by the experts. The clam is usually under the surface in a section of dry sand.

RAZOR CLAM "MINING"

Since the sand is dry and packed, the clam is unable to make effective use of its "suction cup" foot and can move very little. The digger's job is to clear away the sand covering the clam and pick it up. Occasionally this means going down as much as three feet below the surface. This method is sometimes complicated by the fact that the sand, dry on top, is still wet underneath and the clam has its power of locomotion. This situation turns clam digging into a marathon race to see if the clam can dig faster than its pursuer.

BEST BETS

LOCATION: Protected waters in bays and inlets best for bay clams. Small clams found closer to surface; larger clams as deep as 18 inches. Biggest found at lower end of intertidal zone and exposed only during lowest tides.

METHOD: Small shovel or potato fork best. Dig in straight line and sift through sand carefully.

PREPARATION/COOKING: Soak in cold salt water 4-8 hours before cooking. See text for details on preparing/cooking various types.

CHAPTER V
RED TIDE
AND
SHELLFISH
POLLUTION

All of the bivalve shellfish described in the preceding chapters are susceptible to contamination from pollution and the so-called "red tide" organisms.

We can sometimes eat crabs and fish from somewhat polluted environments because we eat only muscle tissue, which often does not contain the polluting material. The exceptions are such long-term pollutants as mercury and other heavy metal poisons.

Shellfish, on the other hand, can be dangerous to eat in polluted waters because we consume the whole animal, including the digestive tract which may contain toxic organisms filtered from the surrounding sea water. It is probably wise to avoid eating shellfish from areas near crowded harbors or boat moorages where human wastes may be pumped overboard. The same holds true for areas where summer homes without proper sewer systems are near the beach.

PARALYTIC SHELLFISH POISONING

This more serious natural poison comes from tiny planktonic

organisms of the gonyaulax family. During the summer months various planktonic organisms will multiply rapidly when water temperature, nutrients and sunlight are present in the right combination.

The organisms become so thick that the water itself sometimes turns reddish brown, giving rise to the popular name "red tide." Most "red tides" are caused by rapid proliferation of harmless plankton and are not dangerous.

The filter-feeding shellfish process these organisms as part of their food supply. When the poisonous gonyaulax are present in large numbers, they become concentrated in the shellfish and can cause serious illness or even death if eaten by man or other mammals. Curiously, they do not harm the shellfish itself.

"Red tide" outbreaks can occur anywhere from April to November in the north Pacific, with most common plankton blooms occurring between May and early September. In more southerly climates where the water remains warmer, plankton blooms can occur over longer periods.

Most shellfish lose their toxins almost completely within four to six weeks after a gonyaulax outbreak. However, the butter clam is a notable and dangerous exception. It can retain the toxic material, especially in the neck of the siphon, for up to two years afer a "red tide" occurrence.

Dr. D.B. Quayle of the Fisheries Research Board of Canada has written an important circular on this subject. With permission from Dr. Quayle, we quote the following information from his Bulletin:

"First, it should be ascertained whether there is a ban in effect on the taking of shellfish in the particular area from which they are to be gathered. Local residents are usually aware of this owing to publicity and, in addition, there are the posted warning signs. If there is a ban in effect, the shellfish specified should not be used under any circumstances.

"If there is no ban, additional protection may be obtained by proper preparation of the shellfish. Unless it is known that the shellfish to be used are entirely safe, they should be cooked fairly well for heat will destroy some of the poison content. The nectar or bouillon from the cooking process should not be used, for any poison in the clam meat, particularly if the siphons are present, will become concentrated in the cooking liquid.

"The butter clam is the most abundant and widely used clam in British Columbia. Recalling the fact that most of the toxin in this species is contained in the siphon and gills, these should be removed before cooking. Thus the butter clam should be opened fresh like an oyster.

EDIBLE PARTS OF CLAM

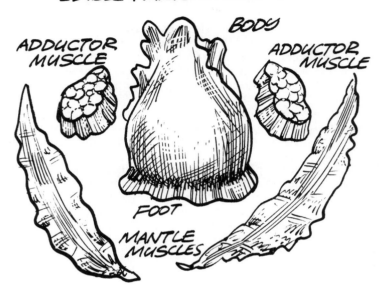

"This then leaves five pieces of meat, the body, two adductor muscles and two mantle muscles. These meats may then be cooked in the usual manner, although chowder preparation causes more reduction of toxicity in butter clams than does frying. Raw clam parts, obtained as described, when compared to similar parts from whole steamed clams are less toxic, so raw shucking of butter clams is recommended.

"It must also be remembered that the amount of toxin, when present, is proportional to the amount of shellfish meat, so the dose of poison is proportional to the amount of meat eaten.

"If these precautions are carefully observed, the risk of being poisoned by clams is very much reduced."

SYMPTOMS OF SHELLFISH POISONING

You are very, very unlikely to have a problem with shellfish poisoning unless you completely ignore all obvious precautions. However, following is a list of some of the symptoms:

The first sensation is usually a tingling and numbness in the lips and tongue, spreading to the extremities of fingers and toes. Difficulty controlling body movements and breathing follow. Artificial respiration might be needed if a case progresses this far.

There is no antidote. Vomiting should be induced with soda, mustard, soapy water, etc. to remove the toxic material from the stomach. The victim should be rushed to the hospital as quickly as possible. If you should be involved in such an incident, keep the balance of your uncooked shellfish and take samples with you for testing. It is possible that the illness is due to another cause which might require a different treatment.

There have been five incidences of shellfish poisoning in B.C. in the last 175 years, and only three of these were fatal. So it is much more likely that clam eaters will die of old age than from shellfish toxicity!

The fisheries departments of the various provinces and states maintain a continuous monitoring program during the summer months. Any sign of gonyaulax is reported immediately, and the news is spread through radio and newspaper announcements and posted notices at marinas and public wharfs.

CHAPTER VI
EXOTIC SEAFOODS

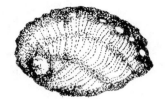

Some types of perfectly edible creatures from the sea are ignored by most harvesters of shellfish and marine life. This is often because they don't look very appetizing and because people don't know how to prepare them.

In this chapter we'll take a look at less popular seafoods such as abalone, limpets, moon snail, sea cucumber, sea urchin, barnacles and various seaweeds. While some readers may choose never to sample any of these delicacies, they are at least worth remembering as valuable sources of protein in an emergency.

Stranded boaters, for instance, could easily locate many of these foods. Even abalone, commonly believed to be found only at great depths, can usually be found on rocks at the lowest tide levels. This univalve is not only large, but also very tasty. Knowing where and when to locate these creatures could make a big difference in an emergency.

ABALONE AND LIMPETS

Limpets and abalones belong to the family of univalves (having only one shell) as opposed to the bivalves (oysters, clams, mussels). Most univalves do not assimilate food by filtering water, as do the oysters and clams. They eat by rasping seaweed with their teeth. This means that they do not take up plankton and are not susceptible to the shellfish poisoning mentioned in the preceding chapter. Neither do they build up concentrations of bacteria, which makes abalone and limpets among the safest of all shellfish to eat.

Other univalves such as the moon snail are carnivorous and can pick up shellfish poisoning second hand. They feed on clams which may be contaminated, and this will be transferred to the predator.

Abalone

This is the most popular of the univalves because of its large size and very tasty meat. It is popular with scuba divers since it can be

found to depths of 100 feet. However, it can also be found on rocks and rock outcroppings near the lowest tide levels.

Gathering from the surface is done primarily during the lowest daylight tides of the year in May, June and July. They can also be gathered during the low night-time tides in November, December and January.

They are found attached to rocky surfaces, usually in areas with good tidal movement. Look on steep, rocky shorelines which contain the seaweed on which the abalones feed. They are often difficult to see because the outer surface of the shell is rough and matches the rocky surface to which it is attached.

Strange as it may sound, it is important to "sneak up" on an abalone so that he can be pulled off the rock quickly. Once an abalone senses your presence, he can grip so tightly with his large powerful muscle that it will be extremely difficult to dislodge him without breaking his shell.

While some abalone hunters use knives, screwdrivers, or even tire irons to pry abalones loose, they are very likely to damage undersized abalone which will die when released. Abalone can be taken by hand or with an "ab iron".

Move quietly to the abalone and insert the "ab iron" quickly under the shell. A quick twist will loosen the abalone before he can squeeze down with his powerful muscle. Be sure to take along a

QUICKLY SLIP SHARP,
FLAT POINT OF "AB IRON"
BETWEEN ROCK AND
ABALONE'S FOOT; TWIST
TO BREAK THE SUCTION.

measuring gauge to check for undersized specimens. They can be made from a piece of plywood cut to the proper size (described in the section on crabs).

Cooking Abalone

Cut the meat from the shell and trim any dark edges. The meat should then be washed in cold water and dried with a paper towel.

ABALONE: SLICE
FOOT INTO
¼"-THICK
"STEAKS";
POUND
THOROUGHLY
TO "TENDERIZE"

It can then be cooked whole, but will have to be pounded with a wooden mallet to break down the sometimes tough muscle fibres. I much prefer to slice the meat across the grain in very thin slices. I sautee these lightly in butter and find them to be tender and delicious. Be careful not to overcook this wonderful delicacy.

Limpets

This "chinaman's hat" shellfish is very small in size, only an inch in diameter. It is usually colored brown or grey to blend in

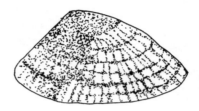

with the rocks to which it attaches itself. It can be found over most rocky beaches attached to the underside of boulders and rocky outcroppings or even concrete sea walls near the high tide mark.

It uses a foot similar to the abalone to cling to the rocks and should also be approached quietly and quickly before it squeezes down tight. Any small knife is suitable for prying limpets off the rocks.

The keyhole limpet lives much closer to the lower end of the intertidal zone. Keyhole limpets are larger and similar to abalone with a small opening at the top of the shell.

Preparing Limpets

Limpets can be eaten raw, although they are quite tough and chewy. They are a favorite food of the Hawaiians after being soaked in a very strong marinade.

Limpets can be steamed in a frying pan like clams (about five minutes) or broiled in the oven. One way to broil limpets is to put a layer of salt in a pan and insert the limpet shell cone side down so that the meat faces up toward the broiler. Adding a few drops of your favorite seafood sauce before broiling adds a gourmet touch.

Limpets can also be cooked in chowders or added to other seafood dishes.

LIMPETS -- SUPPORTED UPSIDE DOWN IN A BED OF SALT

MOON SNAIL

This carnivorous univalve is found near the low tide level where it is a major predator of clams. It is usually necessary to break the

shell to remove the meat. Slice thinly across the grain and pound like abalone to tenderize, then sautee in butter.

The meat has a somewhat unusual taste, and is only for certain palates. However, you can always catch moon snails for their shells, which make a nice decoration. To salvage the shell, it is usually necessary to boil the snail to be able to pull out the meat. Any meat left inside the shell can be removed by leaving the shell on the beach and letting the tiny crabs clean it for you.

SEA CUCUMBER

This creature has the most unappetizing appearance of the edible sea creatures. It is just an elongated blob about the size and shape of a cucumber, brownish yellow in appearance with blunt, yellow spikes all over the body. They are found near rocks and weeds in

71

many quiet water areas where they feed on algae and bottom weeds.

Only a small portion of the sea cucumber is edible. Cut off the ends and shake out the entrails then cut lengthwise and spread the skin out flat. You will find four strips of white muscle which can be cut loose and pulled away from the skin. These should be washed in running fresh water and blotted dry with a towel. The meat can be very tough, so it should be pounded to tenderize and then cut into small pieces and sauteed in butter. It has a mild flavor and a

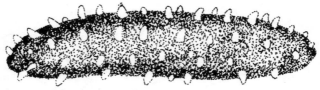

crunchy, crackly texture. I have eaten sea cucumber meat in deep fried fritters and found it delicious.

SEA URCHINS

Sea urchins don't look edible at all. In fact, they look downright menacing with their solid covering of long spiky spines. They are often called the porcupine of the sea.

Urchins can be cleaned by breaking open the bottom center and cutting it loose with a sharp knife. Pull out the bony center and wash off the loose material. The light brown eggs clinging to the sides of the shell form the edible portion of the urchin.

Gourmets eat this raw (like caviar) on crackers. The roe can also be sauteed in butter.

BARNACLES

Yes, barnacles can be eaten! Pry them off rocks with a sharp knife, being careful to cut the meat off the rock as well. Clean off the seaweed and loose shell. They can be eaten raw or placed upside down on a pan covered with rock salt, dotted with butter

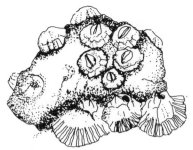

and baked at 350° (for one to two inch barnacles) for about 10 minutes. They taste not unlike oysters.

SEAWEED

Although not as popular in Canada, seaweed is a traditional food in Japan and has become something of an industry in California where as much as 300,000 dry pounds are collected each year.

Many varieties can be eaten raw but most people dry their seaweed, either in the oven or under the sun and eat it as a nibbly snack or use it to enhance salads.

Dulse

This reddish brown seaweed is common all along the seashore and can be easily recognized by its yellow pods which pop when

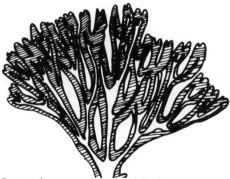

stepped on. It can be eaten raw, with the top two or three inches being the most tender. Avoid the pods or the parts that have started to form pods. It has a bland taste and is chewy with a slightly salty flavor.

After blanching with boiling water, dulse can be dried. Dried, it is a crisp and tasty snack.

Sea Lettuce

As the name suggests, this seaweed looks not unlike a leaf of

lettuce and tastes not unlike a salty lettuce. It can be eaten raw or, blanched and dried, used as a salad seasoner or a snack.

Glasswort

Also known as crowfoot greens or chicken claws, this seaweed is best steamed and seasoned with butter. It is found near the

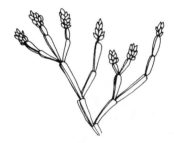

high-tide mark in sheltered inlets, lagoons and bays. Pick the choice green part, leaving some to go to seed. It has a tough inner stem which is discarded but tastes a little like asparagus.

BEST BETS

TIME: Abalone: Lowest daytime tides in May, June and July; lowest nighttime tides in November, December and January.

LOCATION: Abalone: Depths to 100 feet or on rocks and outcroppings near lowest tide levels in areas of good tidal movement.

Limpet: On rocky beaches clinging to underside of boulders near high tide mark (larger keyhole limpet found closer to low tide mark).

METHOD: Abalone/limpet: Act quickly and quietly to prevent either from squeezing down too tight. Pry loose by hand or ab iron.

PREPARATION/COOKING: Abalone: Cut meat from shell and trim dark edges. Slice meat thinly across grain, pound to tenderize. Best sautéed lightly in butter.

Limpet: Leave in fresh water for 30 minutes, cut from shell, sauté in butter. (See text for details on other seafoods.)

Part Two
A Bonanza of Fish

Introduction

When I mentioned to others that I was preparing a book on living off the sea, their first questions always revolved around fish and fishing. While the crabs, oysters, clams, shrimp and other bottom and shore dwelling species are important sources of food, fish are usually considered the most plentiful source of food from the sea.

In the Pacific Northwest salmon is the best known and most sought after species and the first chapter in this section deals with some of the fundamentals of successful salmon fishing. However, for those who truly wish to "live off the sea," there is an almost limitless variety of fish to choose from. Unlike salmon, many of these less sought after fish are easy to catch and in many cases can be taken with simple, inexpensive equipment.

Strictly speaking, not all fish other than salmon are bottomfish — many of those discussed in the following section and classified as bottomfish are in fact mid-water swimmers. But as far as fishing techniques are concerned, we can think of them all in the same category. A general consideration of techniques for bottomfish is detailed in Chapter VIII.

Cod and rockfish (including such delicacies as cabezon and red snapper) are next in line to salmon as most popular fish for the table. In Chapter IX we'll take a look at these fish, their habits and how to catch them. As well as the popular lingcod and red snapper, techniques for taking cabezon, Pacific cod, greenling and rockfish (rock cod), are outlined. All of these fish make excellent eating.

Often overlooked or neglected by anglers, seaperch are one of the easiest to catch fish in B.C. waters. Most varieties, as explained in Chapter X, can be taken either from shore or from piers and breakwaters — there's no need to invest in expensive tackle or boats. These fish are probably the best way to introduce youngsters to fishing. With a little know-how, these fish are easy to catch and can provide hours of family fun.

Very few west coast anglers fish for skate or flatfish; most of those taken are caught by chance while fishing for salmon or cod. While the popularity of these fish has increased somewhat in the last few years, very few fishermen have developed the knowledge and skills required to take them consistently. Chapter XI is a basic guide to these fish.

Dogfish and hake are usually considered the bane of saltwater anglers, but they're often easy to catch and can be made palatable by following the instructions given in Chapter XIII.

While this book is not a survival handbook, the final chapter deals with seafoods that would be relatively easy to obtain by a boater stranded on a beach.

CHAPTER VII
SALMON

No book on living off the sea would be complete without a section on salmon, easily the most popular west coast fish both for the table and from the sportfisherman's point of view. Whole books, including my own *How to Catch Salmon – Basic Fundamentals* and *How to Catch Salmon – Advanced Techniques*, have been written on the subject. Obviously, no single chapter can provide all the detailed information covered in such books.

Instead, I've outlined some of the best, proven techniques for taking salmon. Much of the information is basic to successful trolling and driftfishing for salmon, with one eye always on the "sporting" aspect. As well, there are tips on how to catch salmon when they are feeding on needlefish, the ins and outs of flashers, suitable rods, lines and reels and many other basic aspects of the sport.

Trolling is the most popular method and can be done in anything from a rowboat up to a 100-foot yacht. Trolling means simply drawing a lure behind a moving boat. Consistent success requires persistent dedication and is helped a great deal by some rather sophisticated and expensive equipment. It is possible to catch salmon trolling from a rowboat, but unless you are in the midst of a big run of coho or chinook, your chances of a salmon dinner are relatively low.

A downrigger and a depthsounder are important aids to finding the fish and getting the lures deep enough. Commercial nets and

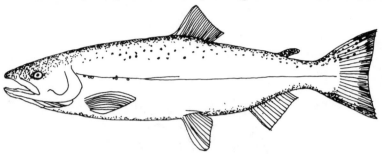

Most often taken trolling, the coho salmon is considered by many to be the top sports fish in B.C.

heavy sport pressure have forced the salmon to run very deep, especially in the heavily fished areas of the inside passage of Vancouver Island, the Strait of Juan de Fuca and Puget Sound.

TROLLING TECHNIQUES

In my opinion, the most successful trolling techniques are as follows:

1. **Use a herring bait**, spoon, or small plug trolled about 15 feet behind the downrigger release clip and about five feet above the downrigger weight. Using this setup, it is important to use a flasher as an attractor hooked on a four to five foot length of 80-pound test leader hooked to the snap swivel holding the downrigger weight.

The flasher swings in a rotating arc (with no lure attached) and attracts fish with its reflective glint and vibrating thump in the water. When using our underwater research camera, we found that more than five times as many salmon came to inspect our lure when we were using the downrigger attractor as when we were not.

Downrigger trolling is deep fishing, and the chinooks are usually found very near the bottom. A good depthsounder with a finely tuned sensitivity adjustment can help you find schools of baitfish and salmon, as well as showing you the bottom itself.

2. **Sandy bottom trolling** — This is a variation of the above technique, but I find it extremely effective for catching salmon when they are feeding on needlefish (candlefish, sandlance) in the late spring, summer and fall.

Use a long, narrow metal spoon which simulates the need-

78

lefish (needlefish lure, Coho King, Koho Killer) or one of my new lures developed from our research with the underwater camera.

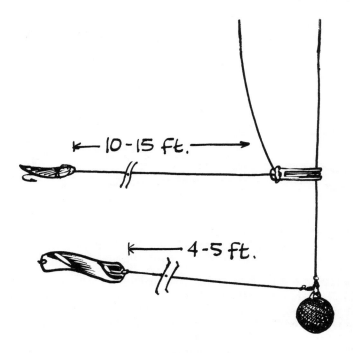

Attach the flasher to the downrigger below the bait on a five-foot length of heavy-test line.

Hooking this lure 20 to 25 feet behind the downrigger clip will allow the weight of the metal spoon to drop it just above the sand where the salmon are feeding.

Drop the downrigger weight until it hits the sandy bottom then crank up one or two turns. Keep "probing" for the bottom by lowering the downrigger weight every few minutes to be sure you are still right on the bottom. The depthsounder will also help you keep close to the sand. Salmon often pick needlefish out of the sandy bottom where they attempt to bury themselves.

I find that adding a tiny bit of bait to the hook on these long narrow spoons adds a great deal to their effectiveness. A piece of herring perhaps ¼" wide by one inch long adds an extra gyrating "joint" similar to the snake-like movements of the needlefish. If the bait dampens the lure action, cut it thinner or use only a piece of skin on the hook.

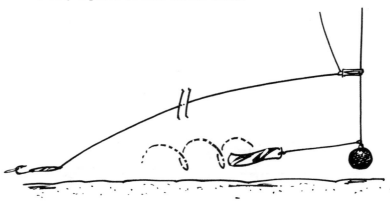

A long narrow spoon with a bit of bait on the hook about 20 feet behind the release clip works when salmon are feeding on needlefish.

3. **Flasher and Hoochie** — I don't particularly care for fishing with flashers on my fishing line, since it takes a lot of the joy out of playing the fish. However, this combination is extremely effective and might be the most productive for a casual angler who is more interested in a salmon barbecue than in the fine points of angling.

A large rotating flasher is usually most effective. Some of the better known brands are Hot Spot, Abe'n Al, B and B, Pal and Nootka. The hoochie is attached on a relatively heavy leader (up to 40-pound test) to give the necessary stiffness so the "kick" of the flasher is transmitted to the lure itself. This gives the lure the erratic side-to-side motion which helps trigger a strike in many instances.

Leader length is a subject of much argument among even expert fishermen. There are no absolute answers, but the manufacturer of each flasher will have recommendations on proper leader length, usually between two and three times the length of the flasher itself. By all means, follow these manufacturers' recommendations; after all, he is interested in helping you catch fish so you will buy more flashers from him!

There are many kinds, sizes and colors of hoochies with such names as Octopus, Twinkle Skirt, Squirt, etc. There are literally hundreds of colors available, and all of them work at certain times. However, the basic colors which are most consistent on a year-round basis are greens, blues, and white. (Pinks and reds are also effective at certain times, especially for pink salmon and sockeye.) It is probably best to ask other fishermen or listen to your CB radio for up-to-date information on the colors which are producing on the day you are fishing.

Flashers are also extremely effective when fished in front of spoons or bait. Use the same or longer leader lengths when using bait. Using plugs with flashers doesn't seem to be productive.

DRIFTFISHING FOR SALMON

Driftfishing or jigging for salmon has increased in popularity by leaps and bounds, especially since the cost of fuel has quadrupled

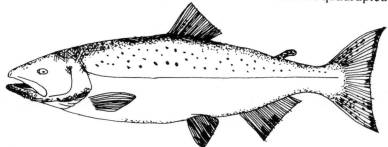

The chinook or spring salmon is often found deep in the water and can be successfully fished either trolling or driftfishing.

in the past few years. Driftfishing is simply casting out or lowering a weighted lure and jigging it up and down. It has many advantages — very low fuel consumption, no smoky, polluting engine exhaust, peace and quiet to enjoy the sounds of nature, and it requires only simple equipment.

If you plan to cast for salmon as well as jig vertically beneath the boat, you will need a good quality heavy duty saltwater spinning reel. An Alvey sidecast reel (made in Brisbane, Australia) is a unique combination of spinning reel and single action reel. It is turned sideways during the cast so that the line peels off the edge of the reel similar to a spinning reel. When retrieving line, the reel is rotated 90 degrees and it acts like a single action reel. (A conventional single action reel or a star drag multiplying reel can be used if you do not plan to do any casting.)

Rods for driftfishing are usually seven to 10 feet in length, depending on the depth you will be fishing. A longer rod with a more limber tip works well when fishing shallow water, but a shorter stiffer rod is needed when fishing deep (up to 100 feet), since the softer pull of the long rod will be absorbed by the stretch in the long nylon line. A hollow fibreglass spinning rod is probably the most suitable rod for driftfishing. It should also be light in weight since you will be holding the rod constantly, and weight quickly becomes an important factor. Graphite and kevlar rods add a stiffer springing action which is helpful in casting, but not so important in trolling.

Monofilament nylon or perlon lines are best for driftfishing even though they have more stretch than is ideal for firm hook setting. Twenty-pound test is certainly adequate; many driftfishermen use 12- or 15-pound test lines. Anything heavier is difficult to cast and the bulk of the line limits reel spool capacity.

Driftfishing Technique

Driftfish lures, unlike trolling lures, work best when fluttering down on a slack line. This is the key to proper driftfishing tech-

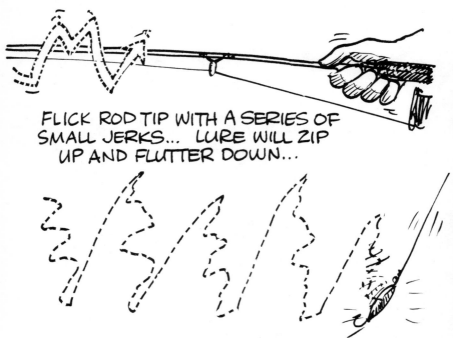

FLICK ROD TIP WITH A SERIES OF SMALL JERKS... LURE WILL ZIP UP AND FLUTTER DOWN...

nique. Some lures, like the Buzz Bomb, rotate rapidly when drifting on a slack line, sending out fish-attracting vibrations.

The lure is lowered to the proper fishing depth, either just above the bottom or just below a school of baitfish. Look for schools of baitfish on your depthsounder, or for schools of diving birds or seagulls feeding on baitfish. Raise the rod tip 18 to 24 inches, then drop it quickly to produce a slack line and allow the lure to flutter down again. Keep repeating this procedure until you feel a bump, tick, or the line feels slack when you start to pull up (this means a salmon may have the lure in its mouth). Then jerk hard to set the hook.

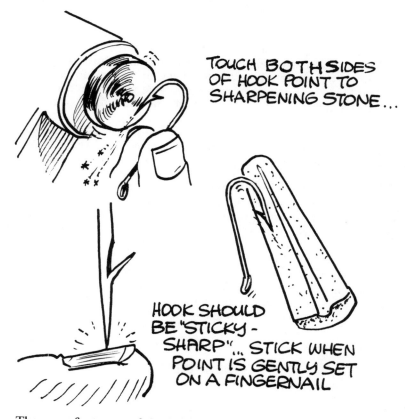

TOUCH BOTH SIDES OF HOOK POINT TO SHARPENING STONE...

HOOK SHOULD BE "STICKY - SHARP"... STICK WHEN POINT IS GENTLY SET ON A FINGERNAIL

The manufacturers of the famous Buzz Bomb lure advise that it is very important not to jerk up too hard on the upstroke, as this often will pull the lure too far away from a curious salmon. A slower, lazier action is more productive.

When casting a drift lure, you should try to place your lure near surface feeding fish, a school of baitfish, or diving birds and seagulls. Allow the lure to sink for perhaps 10 or 15 seconds, then retrieve five or six feet and let the lure flutter down again. Repeat this procedure until the lure is back at the boat.

An alternate method of retrieving is to cast out and reel in as fast as you can crank the reel handle. In certain situations, this technique can be extremely effective, even though it contradicts the basic "slack line" principle. This same fast retrieve method can be used when jigging directly beneath the boat. Simply lower the lure until it hits the bottom, then crank like mad back up to the surface.

The Buzz Bomb is the lure which started the driftfish revolution on the Pacific Coast and is probably still the most popular. Stingsildas, Pirkens, Pirks, Reef Raider, Rip Tide, Mooch-a-Jig, Dart and Zinger are other popular driftfish lures. They come in a wide variety of sizes and colors. As with trolling lures, it is a good idea to try to match the size and shape of the lure to that of the natural feed in the area. Larger and heavier drift lures are needed when fishing in deep water to overcome the effects of tide and current.

I have never believed that color was a major factor in fishing lures, except when surface trolling with bucktail flies. I would suggest you use a lure in the blue, green or silver color spectrum.

One last point about driftfishing: Sticky-sharp hooks are vital to success. Our underwater television camera showed us that fish are striking at our lures more often than we dreamed, but the hooks are often sliding right out of their mouths. This is especially important in driftfishing when the salmon tentatively bites a heavy metal lure on a slack line. Its first instinct is to spit it out, and a sharp hook is much more likely to stick in its mouth. Use a points file, sharpening stone, or an electric hook sharpener to keep hooks sharp.

Jim Gilbert's book *Driftfishing* has all the nitty-gritty details on driftfishing, plus sections on mooching. My own *How to Catch Salmon – Advanced Techniques* has full details on trolling and downrigger fishing.

BEST BETS

Due to the often regionalized nature of salmon fishing, it is best to inquire locally for tips on what salmon are taking and best fishing methods. Look up marina operators, local fishermen and tackle shop owners as well as the preceding chapter and other books such as *How to Catch Salmon* and *Driftfishing*.

CHAPTER VIII
BOTTOMFISH

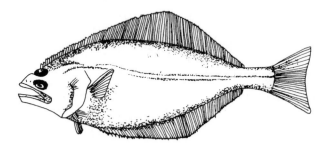

Many readers of this book will be interested in fishing with a minimum of effort and equipment, since their primary goal is food on the table and not entertainment or sport. These people can catch fish by casting from the shore, fishing from a pier or breakwater, or drifting and rowing in a small dinghy or even a raft.

Others will be willing to invest more in equipment and make bottom fishing a hobby or an adjunct to pleasure boating and camping trips.

EQUIPMENT

Either group can choose from the following list of equipment as their interests and budgets dictate:

1. Rods and Reels — my own choice for a single rod and reel for bottom fishing would be a 7½- to nine-foot spinning rod with large guides toward the reel handle and a reasonably stiff butt and medium limber tip. Mooching with live herring or shallow water bait fishing for flatfish might dictate a lighter rod with a more sensitive tip.

An open-face spinning reel (get a heavy duty saltwater model) allows you to cast out from the boat, dock or breakwater, and is also handy for lowering jigging lines to the bottom quickly without drag from a rotating reel.

For trolling, I much prefer a single action "knuckle duster" reel which gives a positive pull on the fish and complete control, as opposed to the slipping clutches of spinning reels and multiplying action star drag reels. Single action reels also allow you to get a good solid direct pull on a heavy stubborn fish, or to work loose from a bottom hangup.

2. Line — A good quality limp monofilament is best for spinning reels with 15-pound test probably the best compromise. Lighter lines can break on a heavy fish or hang up; and heavier lines are often difficult to control on a spinning reel drum. Heavier lines also mean less line capacity on the reel. Dacron line has some advantages for jigging with single action reels since it will not stretch. Hooking small flatfish 100 feet down can be difficult with the 25 per cent stretch factor in nylon line.

3. Depthsounder — I consider this my most important piece of accessory equipment for any kind of fishing, with the possible exception of my downrigger. The depthsounder provides underwater "eyes" so we can learn all kinds of things about the bottom and see concentrations of fish and bait. Today's sophisticated sounders give incredible detail on the composition of the bottom (soft, hard, weed-covered), and real detail on the location and size of bait fish or bottomfish schools.

Some of the newer sounders allow you to zero in on a specific depth. For example, you can set the dial to have the full screen show only 10 or 20 feet of depth at the bottom. This allows the sounder to show schools of fish hanging within a few feet of the bottom where this is impossible on conventional sounders or those which show the entire water column from the bottom to the surface.

4. Fishbox — It is vitally important to have an insulated container to store the catch. Many varieties of bottomfish are quite delicate and should be cleaned and iced as quickly as possible to preserve their texture and flavor. A good insulated cooler is a wise investment.

Some models have compartments to store artificial ice packs in the lid so the coolant is not resting on top of the fish and compressing it. If using ice, I strongly suggest that some sort of screen mesh platform be placed in the bottom of the cooler to keep the fish from the melted ice water which gathers in the bottom of the cooler and softens any fish lying in it. Old refrigerator shelving, aluminum expanded metal, or wooden slats will hold the fish above the drain water.

POSITIONING TECHNIQUES

Much bottom fishing is oriented to a very specific location, often in deep water. Bottomfish schools are often concentrated in very small areas which are difficult to find without marking the locations very accurately.

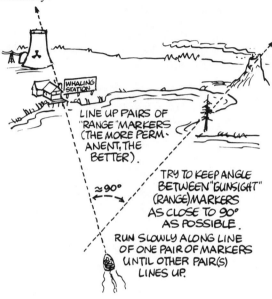

LINE UP PAIRS OF "RANGE" MARKERS (THE MORE PERM- ANENT, THE BETTER).

≈ 90°

TRY TO KEEP ANGLE BETWEEN "GUNSIGHT" (RANGE) MARKERS AS CLOSE TO 90° AS POSSIBLE.

RUN SLOWLY ALONG LINE OF ONE PAIR OF MARKERS UNTIL OTHER PAIR(S) LINES UP.

Taking "gunsight" marks or range markers is the most practical and accurate way to fix your position off shore. Many anglers just look toward the nearest shore line and use only a single point as reference, such as "we were about a quarter mile off shore from the big house with the red roof." This is not very accurate, since you can be anywhere within a several hundred yard radius and still be "off the red roofed house."

Gunsight marks require you to line up two objects on shore (or fixed markers in the sea) which, lined up one behind the other, give you an exact line on which your fishing spot is located. Taking another two objects approximately 90 degrees from the first line gives you an exact spot where the two lines intersect. This method will allow you to know the exact location of your favorite sole bed or red snapper hole, even if it is a mile or more offshore.

I have had problems using anchoring buoys which were subsequently moved and with prominent trees which were subsequently cut down. Large boulders, sharp mountain peaks, buildings, radio towers, and similar objects are good marking objects.

You should also consider the distance and possible poor visibility conditions when you are using hills or distant mountains as part of your marking system.

Once you have marked the exact location of the target fishing area, you will need to consider tide and wind conditions to get the lure to the bottom when the boat is over the exact "hot spot." This is simply a matter of motoring slowly against the wind and tide, with the exact direction dependent on the relative strength of these two elements, and putting the boat in neutral a suitable distance away from the desired fishing hole.

DEEP WATER APPROACH: OPEN REEL AND PAY OUT LINE. DRIFT OVER FISHY AREA, DROPPING LURE AMONG FISH...

At this point the tackle should be lowered quickly as the boat drifts back into the fishing area. Sometimes it takes several tries to get the boat into the proper position so that the tackle reaches the bottom at the proper time.

Shallow water positioning is much easier, since you can simply drop an anchor and pay out anchor line until you are in the proper position.

BEST FISHING TIME

There is no doubt that the best fishing for almost any species is in the early morning. Many fish don't feed actively at night and are hungry in the morning. Fishing in open waters is also more desirable in the mornings because the water is usually calmer.

Some of the flounders and flatfish feed better on an incoming tide, and all deep water fish are easier to catch during slack tide when the water is not moving at all, making it easier to keep the bait over the fish for a longer period. Slack water is also a traditional feeding time for most marine predators.

CHAPTER IX
COD
AND
ROCKFISH

Many of these fish, notably the lingcod, are second only to salmon in popularity among anglers. This is not so much for the sport involved as for the fine eating these fish offer. True seafood lovers often prefer them over salmon. Some gourmands even prefer such fish as cabezon and rockfish over the all-popular lingcod.

Anglers tend to give these fish short shrift, usually resorting to them only when the salmon are not biting or if something is needed for the table. Most west coast anglers do not find them sporting enough. In fact, though, many of these fish can provide fine sport. It's all a matter of method, as we'll see. Even the ignoble rockfish can be a "sporting" fish every bit as exciting as the revered freshwater bass.

LINGCOD

These are among the most aggressive and ferocious of the many bottomfish species. They have large fang-like teeth for catching and tearing their prey. They can grow to 70 pounds with 30-pounders not uncommon. The meat is delicious and they are far easier to fillet than rockfish.

Lingcod are an ambush feeder. They lie quietly in a rock crevice or camouflaged on the bottom, waiting for passing food. Then they will lunge out and grab it in a vise-like grip. Very large lingcod will often grab a rockfish or other bottomfish which is already hooked

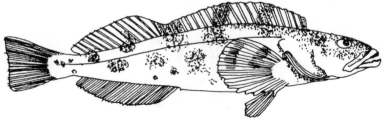

The lingcod is an ambush feeder. Greenling are among the best baits.

and struggling on your line. I have often hooked a small rockfish, sole, or greenling and was reeling it toward the boat when it suddenly stopped as though it had hung up on a reef or other obstruction. Pulling on the rod, the line moves slowly toward the boat, but with a much heavier drag.

If you keep pulling steadily and firmly, the lingcod will hang on to his catch right up to the surface. If you have a landing net or gaff hook ready, you can often gaff or net the lingcod before he lets go.

I sometimes use live rockfish or, better still, a live greenling (which has no spines and is more tempting) as bait for large lingcod. I simply impale the bait on two large hooks, one through both lips and the other through the back near the dorsal fin. The live fish is then allowed to swim down to the bottom where a large ling is often waiting. Keep the baitfish off the rocks by raising the rod periodically to keep him from hiding in a rock crevice. Sometimes a few ounces of weight is necessary to get the rig to the bottom.

CABEZON

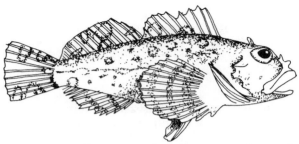

Cabezon make excellent eating but the eggs and entrails are considered toxic.

The Cabezon looks similar to the lingcod with its large, ferocious "toothy" head and mottled brown color, except it is shorter and stockier than the lingcod. It can reach a length of 30 inches and a weight of 25 pounds, but the average weight is about five pounds. It will take many baits and can be caught in shallow water as well as in very deep habitat.

The flesh is a bright greenish blue in color, which is quite a surprise to a first-time Cabezon fisher, but it turns pure white when cooked and is excellent eating.

Warning: The eggs and entrails of this species are considered toxic and should not be eaten by man or animals.

PACIFIC COD

Also known as true cod or gray cod, this bewhiskered species looks almost exactly like the common codfish caught on the East Coast of Canada and the U.S.

Pacific cod prefer a hard-packed sand or mud bottom, but will sometimes be found on sloping, rocky bottoms as well. I have caught most of my Pacific cod at a depth of 125 to 150 feet, but they

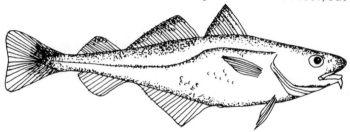

The key to catching Pacific cod is locating the school.

can be taken anywhere from 50 to 200 feet down. They are often caught while trolling deep lines for salmon with downriggers.

They often gather in large schools, hanging 10 to 30 feet off the bottom. Once a school is located, it should be marked precisely and you should end up with a good catch of five- to 15-pounders.

I have caught Pacific cod on herring strip, spoons, plugs and any other bait used for salmon. They are also fond of plastic worms and spoons which are jigged near the bottom while drifting over the fish concentration.

Eating quality is excellent. In fact, Pacific cod have a special meaning for me. While raising my three sons, it was a family tradition for each of us to have our favorite menu on our birthdays. For several years my chosen menu had as its main course a Pacific cod casserole cooked in the microwave oven with a tomato-based sauce.

GREENLING

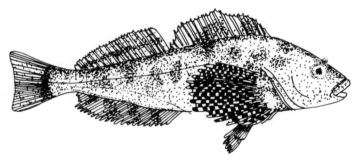

While the name confuses some, greenling is not a lingcod although it makes good lingcod bait.

This name is often confusing to the beginning fisherman because many feel it is a special color of lingcod. In fact, some lingcod are green in color and even have green colored flesh.

However, this is a completely different species with important differences in coloring and body shape. They have very small mouths and soft fins and are not full of spines like rockfish.

There are many different varieties including the kelp greenling, rock greenling, whitespotted greenling and painted greenling. They are called sea trout in many areas, and also kelp cod or kelp trout because of their preferred habitat in kelp beds.

Because of their small mouths, it is a good idea to use a somewhat smaller hook (#2 or #4), and jig with a piece of clam, herring, or pileworm.

They will also strike artificial lures quite readily. I have taken them on small spoons and the plastic jigs mentioned earlier. Some light tackle enthusiasts use a small wet fly which is allowed to sink to the bottom and is retrieved slowly with an erratic action.

Greenling are probably the best bait for large lingcod because of their lack of protruding spines. A two- or three-pound greenling with a large hook through its mouth and another in the dorsal fin is a real killer for lingcod.

Fish are not supposed to have much intelligence, but I was most impressed with the behavior of greenlings in the Undersea Gardens tourist exhibit. I used to watch them work in teams to steal eggs from a female octopus guarding her den. One greenling would nip at the tentacles of the octopus to distract it while another would slip in behind and steal the eggs. These same greenling would often sit on the sills of the underwater windows and we could watch their eyes moving as the spectators walked by the windows. I actually

92

think they were sitting there observing the people just as we were observing them!

ROCKFISH

When I first moved to Vancouver Island in 1956, almost everyone fished for salmon and looked with disdain on "rock cod."

Looked on with disdain by some fishermen, rockfish actually make good eating.

Trolling for salmon, our lures would sometimes get too close to a kelp bed or rocky shoreline where a rockfish would gobble the lure and be thrown back in disgust.

When the salmon weren't biting, I began fishing for rockfish with light tackle, and found it just as sporting as catching freshwater bass. Fileting the carcasses, I found the white, flaky flesh to be excellent eating. In fact, rockfish are a gourmet treat to the Chinese and to many discriminating chefs.

Rockfish are not migratory in the same sense as salmon, so they can almost always be found in suitable habitat. As their name implies, they are usually found on rocky bottoms, hovering motionless in schools a few feet above the bottom. Scuba divers tell me they often see schools of rockfish clustered above the only rocky area within hundreds of yards. Rockfish also hang out in kelp beds and along steeply shelving rocky shorelines.

Rockfish Techniques

Rockfish can be taken by trolling or jigging in these likely spots in exactly the same manner as described for salmon. My favorite method is to tie the bow of the boat to the upstream (or uptide) end of a kelp bed and let the boat drift just along the edge of the kelp. From this position we can cast along the edge of the kelp bed and into the surrounding water where feeding rockfish are likely to be waiting.

For this kind of fishing, I use a small level wind bait casting reel such as those used for freshwater bass. Daiwa, Zebco, Ambassadeur and other brands have a variety of quality models available.

93

A five- or six-foot bass rod and 12- to 15-pound test line completes the outfit. Almost any weighted casting lure will catch fish, but a lead-head jig with plastic worm or multiple plastic tails (some are like a multi-skirted hoochie) are especially effective. (Sebastes Fisheries Company, P.O. Box 10, Kirkland, Washington 98033 have an excellent line of specialty lures for bottomfish.)

The lures are cast out and allowed to sink until they have almost reached bottom, then retrieved in a stop-start motion. Lift the rod tip in a sweeping arc, then drop the rod tip toward the line and reel. Take up the slack before repeating the motion.

Rockfish can also be jigged vertically directly beneath the boat, but this is usually more productive in water deeper than 30 or 40 feet. Sometimes the boat can be anchored to a piece of kelp or to a reef, and the lures allowed to drift with the tidal current away from

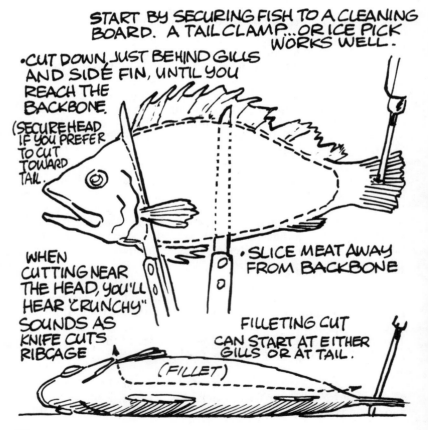

START BY SECURING FISH TO A CLEANING BOARD. A TAIL CLAMP...OR ICE PICK WORKS WELL.

•CUT DOWN JUST BEHIND GILLS AND SIDE FIN, UNTIL YOU REACH THE BACKBONE.

(SECURE HEAD IF YOU PREFER TO CUT TOWARD TAIL.

WHEN CUTTING NEAR THE HEAD, YOU'LL HEAR "CRUNCHY" SOUNDS AS KNIFE CUTS RIBCAGE

•SLICE MEAT AWAY FROM BACKBONE

FILLETING CUT CAN START AT EITHER GILLS OR AT TAIL.

(FILLET)

94

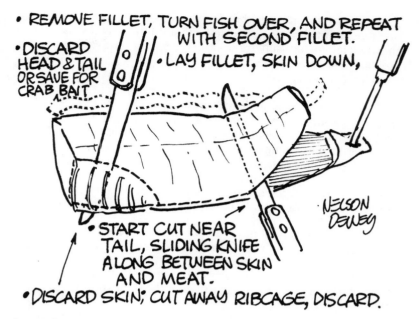

- REMOVE FILLET, TURN FISH OVER, AND REPEAT WITH SECOND FILLET.
- DISCARD HEAD & TAIL OR SAVE FOR CRAB BAIT
- LAY FILLET, SKIN DOWN,
- START CUT NEAR TAIL, SLIDING KNIFE ALONG BETWEEN SKIN AND MEAT.
- DISCARD SKIN; CUT AWAY RIBCAGE, DISCARD.

NELSON DEWEY

the reef and jigged up and down and retrieved much more slowly than in the casting method.

Rockfish can also be taken very effectively by casting from breakwaters, piers, or rocky cliff shorelines. This shore fishing is often extremely effective at night. Many rockfish species, especially black rockfish, come to the surface at night and feed aggressively. They will attack spoons, plugs, jigs and driftfish lures cast from the shore and retrieved with a fast erratic action. This late evening and night fishing is often most productive in late winter and spring before the kelp begins to grow. Casting from shore can be a real problem when the lure must be pulled through a mass of kelp at the end of each cast.

Speaking of black rockfish, this species and the yellow tailed rockfish are not bottom dwellers, but will swim anywhere in the water column and can be found in the same areas where we find salmon or dogfish sharks.

Refining Techniques

Experienced jiggers for rockfish work out all sorts of refinements to their jerking action. Some feel it is best to give several very long, hard jerks to attract fish from a wide area, then follow with a series of short, easy jerks to allow the fish to catch the lure.

Casters often pinpoint the depth at which the fish are feeding by casting out and counting while the lure sinks. They will make a cast at a five count, 10 count, and so forth until they get a strike. Then they will let the lure sink for a similar length of time on future casts to reach the same depth.

"RED SNAPPER"

This is a misnomer, since the red snapper lives on the East Coast and is not found in the Pacific Northwest. The fish we commonly call "red snapper" is one of a number of varieties of red rockfish. They are usually found much deeper than other varieties, and have a bright red color, due partially to their diet of shrimp, red octopus, etc.

Red rockfish are usually found at depths of 100 feet or more, and commercial catches on offshore areas are often as deep as 600 or 700 feet.

They seem to school in very limited areas, probably over some preferred habitat and near a good food source. I have a favorite spot in Patricia Bay near my home in 200 feet of water. However, I must line up my boat very carefully on two sets of "gunsight" shore marks in order to be exactly over the right spot. If I am even 100 feet off the spot, I will catch nothing.

These red rockfish with such names as tambor, bocaccio, canary rockfish and yelloweye, can grow quite large, with many specimens of 15 to 20 pounds or more. The meat is tender and flaky. Many people feel it tastes similar to Dungeness crab.

Since wind and tidal action sometimes make it very difficult to get lures to 200 feet while jigging, I often use my downrigger. I hook it up in the same manner described for sandy bottom salmon trolling, except I use herring strip for bait, then troll very slowly in a circle over the hole.

BEST BETS

LOCATION: Lingcod: Deep, just off or on rocky points and edges of steep drops.

Rockfish: Near bottom in rocky areas; any rocky underwater point; along kelp beds and steeply shelving shorelines.

Red snapper: School in limited areas at 100 feet or more, must be located. Ask locally.

METHOD: Lingcod: Greenling of two to three pounds best live bait, fished near bottom.

Rockfish: Deep trolling or jigging as for salmon. Along kelp beds, drift with kelp casting lead-headed jigs with multiple plastic tails retrieved in start-stop motion.

Red snapper: Herring strip on downrigger to reach bottom.

CHAPTER X
SEA
PERCH

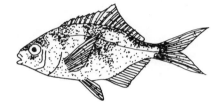

FISHING FROM SHORE

   A boat and motor, while having the obvious advantage of allowing you to move freely, is not a prerequisite of good fishing. Shore
fishing, as we'll see in this chapter, can be very productive in the
surf. Perch fishing from docks and piers in protected bays and
inlets can also be fun and productive.

   Any pier or breakwater which juts out into deeper water can be
an excellent platform from which to fish for a variety of seaperch,
bottomfish and even salmon. It's a relaxed, comfortable style of
fishing, whether you opt for slow and easy bottom fishing with a
baited rig or the slightly more energetic cast-and-retrieve action of
the lure fishermen.

   All of the fish discussed in this chapter can be taken either from
shore or from piers and breakwaters with a minimum of equipment. Almost any rod and reel set-up, a few small hooks, weights
and bait you can easily gather yourself will get you started. In many
cases just a simple handline is all you need.

   Some of the best fishing is to be had in the evenings. I have gone
down to local piers on summer evenings (and also on some quite
crisp fall and spring evenings) to watch happy groups enjoying a

family outing, often cooking up some dinner or hot snack on a small hibachi or camp stove. It's fun and the fishing for various rockfish can really keep things hopping.

SHINER PERCH

Small shiner perch are found in great schools under most docks and piers and have provided fun and excitement to thousands of young boys and girls, often kindling a life-long passion for fishing.

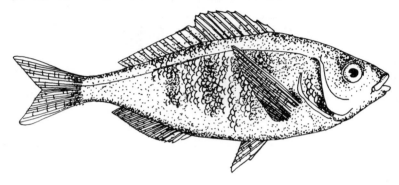

Shiner perch are small but serve to introduce youngsters to fishing.

Most of the really passionate fishermen and fisherwomen, those to whom it is an all-consuming hobby, had their first fishing experience at a very young age. I began fishing with my cousins in small freshwater ponds in Ohio, but I have watched many mothers and fathers teaching sons and daughters the basics of shiner fishing off the floats at marinas up and down the coast.

These shiner perch are too small for eating, measuring from an average three or four inches to a maximum of six inches in length. They are much easier to catch than their larger cousins.

LARGER PERCH

The most plentiful of the larger perch is the pile perch which is dark grey or brown on the back with a silvery luster on the sides and belly. It has dark vertical stripes or blotchy markings on the sides. It can grow quite large, up to 16 inches and 1½ pounds in size. Pile perch give birth to their young alive, often to the startled amazement of youngsters gripping a fresh-caught female and watching a number of tiny, fully formed babies pop out onto the float.

Other popular varieties are the striped seaperch and redtail perch. The striped seaperch is one of the most beautiful fish in the sea. It has a brownish-orange color which seems almost phosphorescent and highly reflective. A series of bright blue horizontal

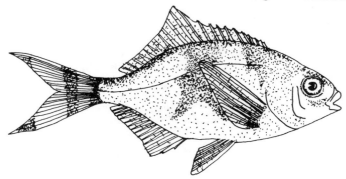

Pile perch are the most plentiful of the larger perch.

stripes along the lower half of the fish and around the head add a striking contrast.

These larger perch are found in the same areas as the small shiner perch, but usually a few feet deeper. They are quite wary of baits and lures, so it takes some strategy and skill to catch them. Dropping a baited lure with a heavy sinker will bring a few lookers, but seldom any strikes. It is usually possible to watch the bait in the water and see the fish investigating it.

CATCHING PERCH

Because perch are such finicky eaters, it is extremely important to present the bait in a natural manner. This means using small hooks (#4 or #5) and a light leader. Some anglers go as light as four to six pounds, but I find 10-pound test is about right. I sometimes also use my normal 20-pound fishing line, then attach a tiny swivel and about five feet of 10-pound leader to the hook.

I prefer to use no sinker at all so the bait falls naturally through the water. This seems to be one of the important keys. Sometimes I will "chum" the water by throwing in some bait without hooks to get the unsuspecting perch in a feeding mood.

I let the bait drop freely to the bottom or through the school of fish. I will let it lie there for a minute or two to see if a curious perch will pick it up, then retrieve and repeat the process.

If there is a tide running under the dock, I will throw the bait up against the tide and let it drift toward me, reaching the proper depth as it passes beneath the dock.

If the fish are quite deep or the current is strong, you can add a couple of small split shot three or four feet from the bait.

Pileworms are extremely effective for perch, but tiny mussels are also excellent, and they form a large part of a perch's natural

Jigging under docks and piers with a handline is an effective way to fish for perch.

diet. The mussel should be broken and threaded on the hook with the pieces of shell still attached. You can also thread a whole mussel with the shell intact (except for the hook puncture).

Also excellent bait are the tiny shore crabs found in great quantities under the rocks near the shore at low tide. They can also be found crawling among the mussels and barnacles on the underside of floats. The small, soft shelled crabs are best, but larger crabs will also take perch. I usually break off the claws of the larger crabs so the perch can eat without risking a split lip. Ghost shrimp, clams and herring are sometimes used, but I find they are not as good as pileworms, mussels, or shore crabs.

This shallow water fishing where you can actually see the fish has both advantages and disadvantages. The perch can see you as well as you can see them, and can be easily "spooked" by sudden movements of your arms or large shapes moving back and forth on

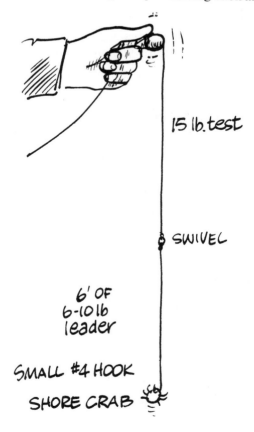

15 lb. test

SWIVEL

6' OF
6-10 lb
leader

SMALL #4 HOOK

SHORE CRAB

The typical perch fishing setup is simple enough even for very young children — and it gets results.

the dock. It is also a good idea to avoid banging and stamping on the float which carries vibrations into the water and scares the fish.

Being able to see the fish allows you to place the bait in exactly the right spot. Sun reflection often inhibits underwater visibility, but if you lie down on the float and look into the shaded area underneath, you will often be able to see a school of perch swimming lazily by. This will allow you to drop the bait in front of them so it flutters down to the right spot.

Perch can be caught at any time of day, but sometimes bite better in early morning or late evening, because this is a natural feeding time for all fish. It is also a quiet time at most marinas.

SURFPERCH

Fishing in the open surf for redtail surfperch, silver surfperch and walleye surfperch requires casting into the surf with a medium

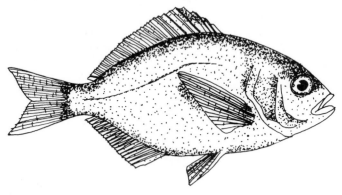

With hip or chest waders and the proper gear, surfperch can be caught in the open surf.

to heavy action spinning rod seven to 10 feet long. It should be fairly stiff to give a good "snap" on the cast. A heavy duty saltwater spinning reel is best, but large bait casting reels are also suitable.

LEAD WEIGHT, CAST IN BOWL OF A SPOON; DRILLED; WIRE LOOPS ATTACHED

Use about 15-pound test line, which should be thin and soft enough for good spin casting, yet strong enough to stand up in the heavy surf conditions. A #4 to #6 hook baited with pileworms, ghost shrimp, or clam necks works well. It sometimes helps to add a bit of color with a bright red bead or even a small metal spinner in cloudy surf conditions.

Hip or chest waders will be needed to allow you to wade into

Surfperch hookups

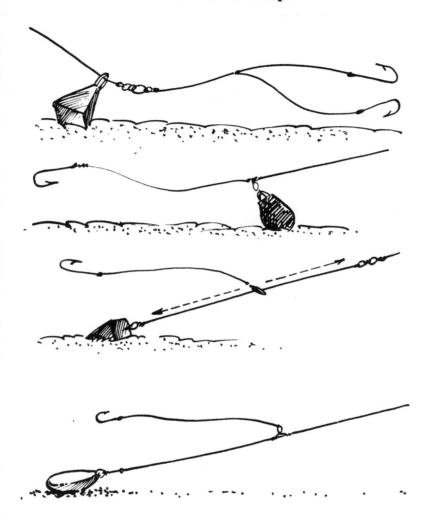

Various hookups can be used for surfperch, but a 15-pound test thin casting line, #4 to #6 hooks and a sinker of two to four ounces works best. The sinker must be heavy enough to hold the bait on bottom in heavy surf. Pile worms and clam necks make good bait.

shallow water and get more distance on the cast. Hardy souls sometimes wade into the surf in bare feet or tennis shoes on warm summer days.

A sinker of two to four ounces is needed to hold the bait on the bottom in the heavy surf. This can be either pyramid shaped or dish shaped. Pyramid sinkers are available in most sporting goods stores, but the dish sinkers can be cast yourself by using large tablespoons or serving spoons as a mold and filling them with molten lead. Then simply drill a hole in one end and attach a snap-swivel. The dish-shaped sinkers don't hold the bottom quite as well as the pyramid sinkers, but are much easier to retrieve, and you will experience less frustration with hangups. Simply pull the rod up sharply (just the same action as setting a hook) to free the dish sinker from the sand.

Surfperch are aggressive feeders, and are very plentiful along most stretches of open beach. They feed primarily on an incoming tide and often concentrate on small depressions or rivulets where fresh water has carved a trough at low tide. If you observe these areas during low tide conditions, you can concentrate on them when the tide comes in.

BEST BETS

LOCATION: Pileperch: Under docks and piers beneath schools of smaller shiner perch.
    Surfperch: Open beaches with good surf.
METHOD: Pileperch: Small hooks, light line baited with pileworms, small mussels, shore crabs and fished on bottom.
    Surfperch: On incoming tide cast small spinner baited with pileworms, clam necks into surf and let settle to bottom. Look for depressions caused by fresh water.

CHAPTER XI
SKATE
AND
FLATFISH

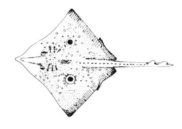

Skate are members of the shark family and are also related to the stingrays and batrays of tropical waters. They are large, flat, diamond shaped animals who feed almost exclusively on the bottom and can grow to huge sizes. We captured a specimen for the Undersea Gardens that was more than six feet across and weighed well over 100 pounds.

Skate are often captured by scuba divers who grasp them at the forward end of their "wings" and hang on for a thrilling ride across the bottom. When the skate exhausts itself, he can be dragged up on the beach. Skate can be captured by hook and line, but most are caught accidentally while fishing for other species. They feed on clams, herring, seaworms and any other natural bait. They sometimes cruise around under marina floats, feeding on fish entrails discarded by fishing boats.

They also feed on small crabs. We had a fascinating experience at Sidney Spit off Vancouver Island while studying crabs entering crab traps with our underwater television camera. We saw a huge skate approach our trap and attempt to get at the crabs inside by poking his large snout into the entrance tunnel, but his size (probably four feet across) prevented him from getting in. He gave up after three attempts.

HOOKING SKATE

If you hook a skate, set the hook and let him run. He may peel off several hundred feet of line, but will eventually tire and can be

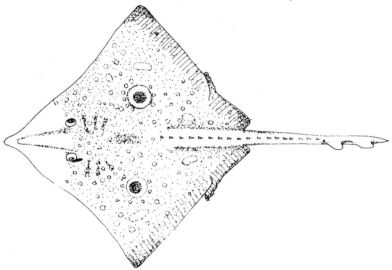

Skate will peel off several hundred feet of line when hooked, but if allowed to run will eventually tire. Use a gaff for pulling out of the water.

worked to the dock. A stiff gaff hook is best for pulling the skate onto the dock, or it can be worked to the nearest shoreline and skidded up on the beach.

Skate makes delicious eating. Filets from skate "wings" are often sold in fish markets. More imaginative marketers cut circular "plugs" one to 1½ inches in diameter from the wings and market them as a substitute for scallops. Many seafood casseroles contain round skate wing fillets that most diners cannot distinguish from scallops.

FLATFISH

The term flatfish refers to the wide range of fish which have both eyes on the same side of their body and lie flat on the bottom. It includes many varieties of sole, flounder, halibut, turbot, plaice, brill and sand dab. These flatfish are a remarkable example of Darwin's theory of evolution and survival of the fittest. All flatfish are adaptations of the more common upright swimming fish like saltwater perch or freshwater bluegills.

Biologists speculate that millions of years ago some fish found that lying flat in the sand or mud would help them hide from their

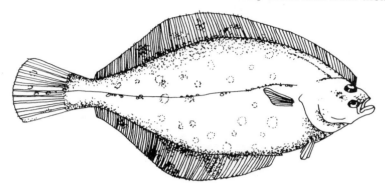

Flatfish such as the sole are ambush feeders and must be located precisely to be fished successfully.

enemies and provide a handy point of ambush. Mutations and variations gradually developed to change the shape and position of the fins. In an evolutionary miracle, one eye actually migrated to the other side of the head so that the fish could feed much more efficiently. All flatfish begin life with eyes on both sides of their body, but one eye moves to the other side of the head at an early stage of their growth.

A parallel evolutionary development was the development of camouflage skin coloring and patterns. They can settle to the bottom and cover their bodies with a thin layer of sand or mud by a couple of quick movements of their fins, making them almost invisible to predators or prey.

Fishing Techniques

Since all flatfish tend to be ambush feeders, lying hidden and camouflaged waiting for suitable food to drift by, it is vital to be in exactly the right location. In fact, pinpointing flatfish "beds" is the most important single factor to fishing success. They are all active feeders, and will take almost any natural bait if it can be presented close to their habitat.

I used to think that sandy bottoms were best for most kinds of flatfish, but I have learned that most of them prefer a mud bottom. Sandy bottoms tend to be more sterile without the nutrients found in the mud. Tiny organisms feed on these nutrients and are in turn eaten by larger organisms, continuing the food chain and providing protein for the carnivorous flatfish.

Locating these fertile areas is often a matter of trial and error,

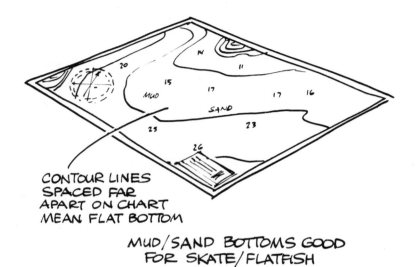

CONTOUR LINES
SPACED FAR
APART ON CHART
MEAN FLAT BOTTOM

MUD/SAND BOTTOMS GOOD
FOR SKATE/FLATFISH

but there are some shortcuts. The best is to talk to local "old timers" to see if they will share their secret spot with you. You can also get some tips from studying marine charts. Ideal location would be a mud bottom with a very gradual slope. (Gradual slopes are indicated on charts by wide distances between the depth contours on the chart.) Flatfish can be found at depths from 15 feet to 150 feet or more.

Once a productive spot is found, it should be marked with the precision of a hidden treasure, because that's exactly what it is. Take exact "gunsight" marks in two directions and some extra ones just in case. As I described in my book *How to Catch Bottomfish*, I had located some extremely productive sand dab feeding grounds, and used some navy anchoring buoys to pinpoint the spot. One morning I woke up to find the buoys had been moved and it took me many frustrating trips to find the spot and re-mark it.

As with other still fishing techniques, you can anchor the boat over the "hot spot" if the water is less than 40 or 50 feet deep. If the water is deeper, you will need to position the boat upcurrent and upwind from the fishing location, then drop the lines quickly to the bottom as you drift over the spot.

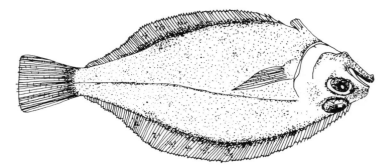

Once a school of sand dab is located, fishermen should mark the spot carefully for future reference.

Raise and lower the rod slowly so that you bump the bottom every few feet. You will know quickly when you are in the right spot, because flatfish bite aggressively and you will feel the sharp frantic tugs of one or more sole, sand dab, etc. Set the hook with a

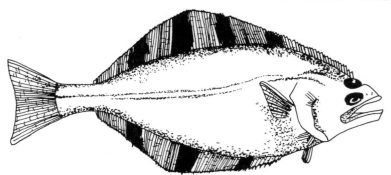

Slowly trolling a spinner and worm combination will often result in a good catch of flounder.

short jerk and enjoy playing the fish on your light spinning rod.

Spinning rods are ideal for deep water drifting for flatfish, since you can cast the line upcurrent of the spot and let the line peel rapidly off the edge of the reel spool with no resistance to slow its descent to the bottom.

Deep water fishing is usually best near slack tide because this is the natural feeding time for fish, and it is also the easiest time to hold the bait over the fish concentrations. A flooding tide is best in

109

Flatfish hookups

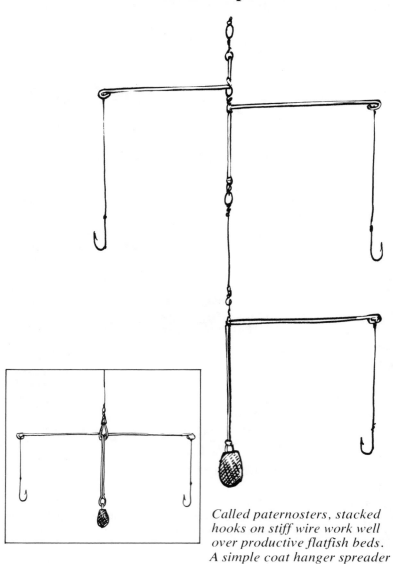

Called paternosters, stacked hooks on stiff wire work well over productive flatfish beds. A simple coat hanger spreader (inset) holds two hooks apart with a sinker in the middle.

shallow water fishing for flatfish. Flounder often move into shallow water on a flooding tide to feed on small crabs, clams and other inter-tidal organisms.

Generally speaking, the larger flatfish will be in deeper water,

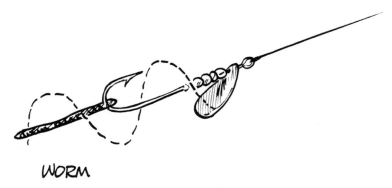

WORM

While herring strips and chunks of clam are good flounder bait, a simple worm and spinner combination often works best.

although some predatory flatfish will actually be feeding on the smaller ones. I have caught large petrale sole up to six pounds in the midst of a school of small sand dabs.

Large flounder can be taken by slow trolling, usually by putting the boat in and out of gear. Spinners and worms are a very successful combination, although herring strip and chunks of clam can also work well. Gang-trolls used for trout are also successful for flounder, but many of them offer too much drag on the line and prevent it from getting deep enough. The lures must be kept very close to the bottom.

Rowing in a small dinghy is an excellent exercise and a great way to catch flounder. The intermittent action of the oars gives an erratic movement to the bait. Slow trolling by rowing backwards so that the blunt end of the boat slows forward progress also works well.

Flatfish rigs

Since flatfish beds can be so productive, I often use more than one hook on the line and catch two at once. A simple coat hanger spreader holds two hooks apart with a sinker in the middle. Other rigs employ hooks "stacked" vertically on the line with stiff wires holding them away from the main line. These are called paternosters.

Another popular rig is a ledger, where the sinker slides on the line with the hook dangling free. This has the advantage of allowing small fish to grab the bait and run off without feeling any resistance from the sinker.

Hook sizes should be scaled to the likely size of the fish. I use #4 or #6 hooks for the small sand dabs in Patricia Bay near my home, but hooks up to #1 can be used for large flounder and even larger hooks for petrale sole and brill.

BEST BETS

SKATE: Once hooked, allow skate to run until tired. Clams, herring, seaworms make good bait.

FLATFISH: Prefers mud bottoms, best fished at slack tide, study marine charts, ask locally. Active feeders, will take most baits but school must be located.

CHAPTER XII

HALIBUT
KING
OF THE
FLATFISH

These giants are in a class by themselves. They grow to enormous size with specimens over 100 pounds common, and a number of 200-pounders taken each year, but they are not easy to catch. Persistence can pay big dividends: one halibut of 100 to 150 pounds will fill the freezer for an entire year. Some consider them the finest eating fish in the sea.

Halibut can be found on large sand or mud banks off the open coast, and sometimes in shallow inlets and bays. They tend to migrate to inside waters in the spring when many salmon anglers are surprised to hook into one of these underwater freight trains.

Halibut are often found on the top of "seamounts," underwater plateaus of shallow water surrounded by much deeper water. A team of fisheries researchers working near the Bowie Seamount off the Queen Charlotte Islands caught specimens up to 200 pounds using chrome-plated Norwegian cod jigs.

Halibut will eat almost any bait and attack any salmon lure. Many are caught on cut-plug herring by salmon anglers fishing near the bottom. You can also use live perch, rockfish, or greenling as halibut bait. They should be rigged alive with large hooks (one through the mouth and one through the side or dorsal fin area). Frozen baits are also successful. Commercial fishermen use frozen squid, octopus and Pacific cod on their set lines.

Halibut are even reputed to eat whole salmon. They will move

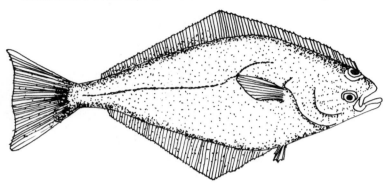

Large halibut can be dangerous in a small boat. Such fish should be tied to the boat and towed ashore.

into the river mouth areas in south-east Alaska in the fall when the salmon are gathering to make their spawning migrations. I have heard stories that some of these monsters weigh as much as 500 pounds and gobble up whole sockeye and pink salmon.

They are a very powerful fish and can be dangerous in a small boat. In fact, there are signs on the docks in Juneau and Ketchikan, Alaska warning boaters not to bring large halibut aboard boats, especially wooden boats. The powerfully muscled fish will sometimes thrash about and pound his powerful tail against the bottoms and sides of a boat, smashing the planking. Some boats have been sunk with tragic loss of life.

Large halibut should be played out beside the boat, then attached to a piece of mooring line or anchor line and towed slowly to shore. Some halibut fishermen carry a small rifle and shoot the fish in the head before attempting to land it or handle it. Many are landed with conventional salmon tackle and plenty of 20-pound monofilament line. However, some anglers who target specifically on halibut will use 40-pound test nylon line.

BEST BETS

LOCATION: Prefers large sand or mud banks. Moves into inside waters in spring, found on seamounts surrounded by much deeper water.
METHOD: Not easy to catch as difficult to locate, but will take most baits including salmon lures. Use 40-pound test line. Do not attempt to boat larger fish as can damage boat.

CHAPTER XIII
THE
"UNDESIRABLES"

Hake and dogfish sharks are usually considered the most undesirable fish in the sea by sportfishermen. Hake are considered undesirable because of their tendency to go "soft" soon after they're caught; dogfish because of the unpleasant flavor of the flesh — and just the fact that they are sharks.

Very few anglers seek them out; those that are caught are usually taken while fishing for something else and are either killed and discarded or just thrown back. In fact, though, both these "undesirable" fish can be excellent for the table. That's right, both dogfish and hake are good eating. The key is in handling them properly once they're caught.

HAKE

This somewhat unattractive fish has large eyes and a mouth full of long, needle-sharp teeth. They are disdained by most salmon fishermen when they are caught inadvertently by trollers. In fact, they are usually thrown back with the same disgust as a dogfish shark.

However, hake are a most delicious eating fish when cared for properly. This is the same fish that is known on the East Coast as whiting and is popular with both sport and commercial fishermen. Russian and Japanese commercial trawlers catch them in great quantities for home consumption and for export back to Canada and the U.S. where they are often sold as "fillet-of-fish." It is

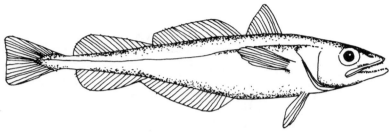

Properly cared for, hake make excellent eating. They are often sold as "fillet-of-fish."

likely that you have eaten hake in a fish sandwich at your favorite fast-food restaurant. Biologists estimate that approximately 375 million pounds of hake can be harvested annually without hurting the resource.

Hot Stomachs

The big problem with hake is their tendency to go soft very quickly, due to what is known as a "hot" stomach. This is due to their diet which involves food items that decompose rapidly. Hake should be filleted as quickly as possible after capture and iced in a cooler. They should not be left in melted ice where the water will cause the flesh to soften.

Hake are voracious feeders and will take almost any of the baits used for salmon or bottomfish. They are a deep water fish (the large eye helps them see in low light levels) often caught at 150 feet or deeper and are usually found in large schools. Once located, it is relatively easy to get a large catch of two to four pound specimens.

DOGFISH SHARKS

This is undoubtedly the most disliked fish in the entire North Pacific. It steals the bait from salmon fishermen, bites off their line and lures, and sometimes makes still fishing with herring or live bait almost impossible. Dogfish are members of the shark family, with the same streamlined shape and razor sharp teeth as their larger man-eating cousins. Shark has become a popular seafood dish, and dogfish are as good eating as any of the shark family.

As any salmon fisherman will tell you, dogfish will eat anything. They prefer herring and other natural baits, but they will also take artificial lures and even bucktail flies. Biologists in Washington

State examined dogfish stomach contents and found 77 different organisms including several types of fish, worms, clams, starfish, crabs, squid, sponges, jellyfish and snails.

I had one frustrating experience with Bruce Colegrave, author of the best selling book, *Bucktails and Hoochies*. We were having a marvelous morning fishing for coho salmon on a bright September

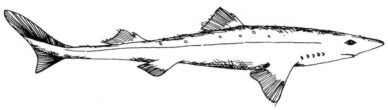

The bane of anglers, dogfish can be eaten if soaked in vinegar overnight.

day in Saanich Inlet near my home. We were trolling bucktail flies with mother-of-pearl spinners right on the surface and had four beautiful coho in the boat. The screaming reel announced another strike, and Bruce played a 12-pound coho up beside the boat. Just as I prepared to net it, a huge dogfish rushed up and seized the bucktail fly in the salmon's mouth. There was a lot of frantic thrashing, and the dogfish came away with the fly and hook in its mouth. The big hook-nosed coho, suddenly free of the lure, swam away before we could net it. This was probably the ultimate frustration, exchanging our lovely coho for a dogfish right beside the boat!

WHERE TO FIND DOGFISH

Dogfish are mid-water swimmers but can be found anywhere from the surface to the bottom. They are usually found near schools of herring or other baitfish. In the fall of the year, the large pregnant females gather in protected bays and inlets to have their young.

After finding a school of dogfish, it is usually easy to entice them to strike. The biggest problem is to keep them from biting off your line and lure, so a wire leader attached to the lure is important.

When landing a dogfish, be careful of the sharp teeth and spines at the forward end of the dorsal and adipose fin. A pair of heavy gloves is handy for holding the fish while removing the hook with long-nose pliers. Be careful of the spikes as they can jab through even heavy canvas gloves. Sharp blows to the head with a club or fish billy will usually quiet a thrashing dogfish, but I find it more effective to make a quick surgical cut behind the head deep enough to sever the spinal chord.

If you are anchored in a bay or inlet, it is often possible to attract dogfish by throwing fish carcasses over the side in shallow water and waiting for 10 minutes to an hour.

My three sons and their friends used to have some great fun fishing for dogfish off the small dock in front of my home. When I returned from a fishing trip, they would take the salmon heads and bottomfish carcasses and throw them off the end of the dock in the late evening. Later, they would shine their flashlight into the water and watch the dogfish swarming around the carcasses. Then they would drop a heavy cod jig or herring on a wire leader and jig it up and down, catching dogfish almost immediately.

We never ate the fish in those days, usually saving them for fertilizer for the garden, but dogfish are extremely popular in Europe, England and in the Orient. It is sold as ''rock salmon'' in England, and is the major ingredient in many fish and chips dinners. It is also filleted in long strips and sold in France and Germany as a type of eel.

PREPARING DOGFISH

The major problem with eating dogfish is the unpleasant ammonia odor and taste in the flesh. Most members of the shark family have a high concentration of blood-urea due to a pecularity in their gill structure. Evidently the gills are not permeable to urine as with other fish, and some unpleasant byproducts collect in the flesh.

Dogfish gourmets have found the ideal answer to this problem. Soaking dogfish fillets in a weak solution of vinegar or lemon juice will completely eliminate any urea or ammonia taste or smell after an overnight soak.

BEST BETS

HAKE: Fillet immediately and place in cooler. Found at depths of 150 feet and deeper. Will take any bait fish. Found in large schools; easy to catch once located. Ask locally.

DOGFISH: Found anywhere in the water column near schools of bait fish. Use wire leaders, any bait works. Chumming can draw large schools. Soak fillets in weak solution of vinegar and lemon juice overnight to remove ammonia taste.

CHAPTER XIV
SURVIVAL

It seems that the number of boaters who find themselves in trouble goes up with frightening regularity every year. Often it's nothing more than a conked-out engine and an unpleasant wait until someone comes along with a towline. Other times, though, it's a case of an undersized boat tackling water it was never designed to take. In some sea conditions even the best-equipped, most cautious boater can suddenly face disaster. It's in these cases that real trouble can strike and when a working knowledge of "living off the sea" can turn from fun to dead earnest.

I said at the outset that this is not a survival book. Readers should not consider it a handbook for coping with emergency conditions. However, many of the techniques and tips outlined could come in handy in any number of basic survival situations. The following information could be used by boaters, sportfishermen or others, who for one reason or another find themselves stranded on a beach. This chapter deals only with easy-to-obtain foods which could help in such situations; boaters are urged to consult other sources for information on survival skills and what to do in an emergency at sea.

Crabs

While crabbing is best done out of a boat using traps, crabs can often be picked by hand in shallow waters. The key is finding the right spot, one with suitable crab habitat.

The Dungeness or sand crab is the most plentiful along the

In the right spot crabs can be found in shallow water with sandy bottoms.

Pacific coast. Look for them in sandy bottom areas with good tidal movement, especially areas with eel grass or near river mouths. They can often be found by wading the shallows in such areas. At low tide they are buried in the sand or hiding under seaweed.

Shrimp and prawns

Most shrimp and prawns are found in deep water and can only be taken using traps. However, from August through November the coon stripe shrimp, one of the most plentiful, migrates into shallow water in the evenings.

Look for them after dark, especially in the very early morning hours. A flashlight is a great help as the shrimp eyes glow brightly in its light. Simply scoop them up and boil in salt water.

Oysters

The best place to look for oysters is in quiet bays and backwaters with warm water temperatures. They are found between the high and low tide marks. Easiest way to cook is in the embers of a beach fire. Place them on the embers with rounded shell down until a slight gap is visible between the shells.

Clams

Smaller clams are found close to the surface; larger clams are deeper and closer to the low tide mark. Look for them in protected waters such as bays and inlets. Lacking a shovel, dig for them with a paddle or stick. Soak them in salt water for four to eight hours to remove sand and grit. They can be stored on a bed of seaweed and covered with more seaweed. Moisten periodically. Steam them by placing in a container with about two inches of water, bring to boil and let simmer 30 to 40 minutes.

Abalone

Usually found at depths of 100 feet or more, but you can sometimes find them during the lowest tides of the year clinging to rocks

Usually found deep in the water, abalone can also be found at low tide clinging to rocks.

and rock outcroppings. In particular, search steep, rocky shorelines which contain seaweed; abalone feeds on seaweed. Use stealth; if it senses your presence it will clamp down tight. To cook, cut away from shell, trim dark edges, slice across the grain and fry.

Limpets

Often called the "chinaman's hat", they can be found on most rocky beaches attached to the underside of boulders near the high tide mark. Like abalone, if it senses your presence it will clamp down too tight to be easily removed. Can be eaten raw or steamed like clams.

Barnacles

You'll need a sharp knife to pry them off of rocks along the beach. Be careful to cut the meat off the rock as well. They can be eaten raw.

Sea cucumber

Only a small portion of this spiky creature can be eaten. Look for them near rocks and weeds in quiet water. They feed on algae and

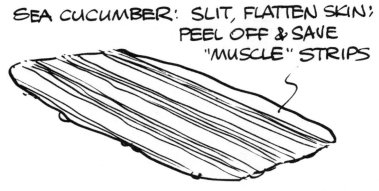

SEA CUCUMBER: SLIT, FLATTEN SKIN; PEEL OFF & SAVE "MUSCLE" STRIPS

bottom weeds. Cut off the ends and shake out entrails then cut lengthwise to expose four strips of white muscle. This meat can be tough and should be rinsed in fresh water.

Sea urchin

This porcupine of the sea can be eaten by breaking open the bottom center to expose the light brown eggs clinging to the sides of the shell. The eggs can be eaten raw.

Seaweed

Various types of seaweed are edible. Among the easiest to obtain are dulse and sea lettuce. Dulse, a reddish brown seaweed found almost everywhere (easily recognizable by its yellow pods) is good raw. The top two or three inches are best. Can also be set in the sun to dry. Sea lettuce, easily recognized by its similarity to a leaf of lettuce, can also be eaten raw or dried.

Fish

A minimum of equipment — hook and line — is required before fish can be taken. Even then, most species will be beyond reach of a stranded boater without a useable boat. There are fish, however, which can sometimes be taken either from shore (or by wading into slightly deeper water) or from rocky points of land which jut out into deep water.

Surfperch can be caught on a hook baited with clam necks and allowed to settle to the bottom in fairly shallow water just off the beach. They are plentiful along most stretches of open beach and feed primarily on incoming tides. They often congregate in small depressions carved by entering fresh water.

Greenling can also be taken with a piece of clam as bait if you can reach the kelp beds these fish frequent.

Rockfish are more difficult to catch from shore but can some-

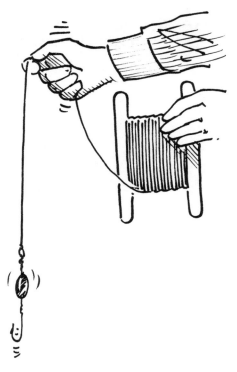

A simple handline rig can be an effective way to catch small fish in an emergency.

times be taken off long rocky points where there is a rocky bottom or near a kelp bed. Steeply shelving rocky shorelines can also be tried. Some sort of lure jigged as for cod will generally work. If bait fish are available, use them. Night fishing is best as this is the time they come to the surface to feed.

The same areas can also be fished with shore crabs or clam parts as bait for a variety of perch. Perch are finicky eaters and should be fished with caution.

Learning to live off the sea should be both fun and exciting as well as providing excellent food for the table. In an emergency the information in this last chapter can be useful, but hopefully you'll never have to use it in that way.

Far better that you go prepared and venture only in areas suitable to the type of boat you're using. In fact, you could "live off the sea" without ever stepping into a boat, as we've seen in many sections of this book.

Have fun, enjoy the many seafoods you've learned to harvest and keep conservation in mind.

A selection of other HERITAGE HOUSE titles:

Heritage House books are sold throughout Western Canada. If not available — or for a free 16-page catalogue listing 150 titles — write: Heritage House, Box 1228, Station A, Surrey, B.C. V3S 2B3. Shipped postpaid in Canada. Payment can be by cheque or money order.

The PIONEER DAYS IN BRITISH COLUMBIA Series

Every article is true, many written or narrated by those who, 100 or more years ago, lived the experiences they relate. Each volume contains 160 pages in large format magazine size (8½ x 11″), four-color covers, some 60,000 words of text and over 200 historical photos, many published for the first time.

A continuing Canadian best seller in four volumes which have sold over 75,000 copies. Each volume, $8.95

WHITE SLAVES OF THE NOOTKA

On March 22, 1803, while anchored in Nootka Sound on the West Coast of Vancouver Island, the *Boston* was attacked by "friendly" Nootka Indians. Twenty-five of her 27 crew were massacred, their heads "arranged in a line" for survivor John Jewitt to identify. Jewitt and another survivor became 2 of 50 slaves owned by Chief Maquina, never knowing what would come first — rescue or death.

The account of their ordeal, published in 1815, remains remarkably popular. New Western Canadian edition, well illustrated. 128 pages. $8.95

LOWER MAINLAND BACKROADS:

This best selling series contains complete information from Vancouver to the southern Cariboo. Each volume contains mile-by-mile route mileage, history, fishing holes, wildlife, maps, photos and much other information.

Volume One — Garibaldi to Lillooet, Bridge River Country. $9.95
Volume Two — The Fraser Valley. $2.95
Volume Three — Junction Country: Boston Bar to Clinton. $9.95

OUTLAWS AND LAWMEN OF WESTERN CANADA

These true police cases prove that our history was anything but dull. Chapters in 160-page Volume Three, for instance, include Saskatchewan's Midnight Massacre, The Yukon's Christmas Day Assassins, When Guns Blazed at Banff, and Boone Helm — The Murdering Cannibal.

Each of the three volumes in this Canadian best seller series is well illustrated with maps and photos and four-color photos on the covers. Volume One, $7.95; Volume Two, $7.95; Volume Three, $9.95

B.C. PROVINCIAL POLICE STORIES: Mystery and Murder
from the Files of Western Canada's First Lawmen

The B.C. Police, born in 1858, were the first lawmen in Western Canada. During their 90 years of service they established a reputation as one of the most progressive police forces in North America. All cases in this best selling title are reconstructed from archives and police files by ex-Deputy Commissioner Cecil Clark who served on the force for 35 years.

Sixteen chapters, many photos. 128 pages. $7.95

THE DEATH OF ALBERT JOHNSON: Mad Trapper of Rat River

Albert Johnson in 1932 triggered the greatest manhunt in Canada's Arctic history. In blizzards and numbing cold he was involved in four shoot-outs, killing one policeman and gravely wounding two other men before being shot to death.

This revised, enlarged edition includes photos taken by "Wop" May, the legendary bush pilot whose flying skill saved two lives during the manhunt. Another Canadian best seller. $7.95

FORT STEELE: Here History Lives

From a thriving 1890s community that called itself "The Capital of the Kootenays," Fort Steele declined to a ghost town. But it was reprieved when the B.C. Government began a restoration program which now attracts some 300,000 visitors a year.

Here in 50,000 words with over 100 photos and four-color covers, Fort Steele lives again. 160 pages. $9.95

TRAGEDIES OF THE CROWSNEST PASS

In Canada no place equals the tragedies which have buffeted the Crowsnest Pass on the B.C.-Alberta border. At Frank a mountain collapsed, killing nearly 100 people; at nearby Hillcrest 189 miners died in a mine disaster; at Fernie another explosion killed 128 miners and a massive fire left virtually every resident homeless.

Revised edition of a Canadian best seller. 96 pages. $6.95

THE BEST OF B.C.'s HIKING TRAILS

Here are 20 great hikes from all around B.C. to suit hikers of all levels of ability. Each hike is accurately described and mapped and you'll find complete details of how to get there and what you can expect to find.

Illustrated throughout with photographs, this is essential reading for all hiking enthusiasts. 174 pages. $9.95

GHOST TOWNS AND DROWNED TOWNS OF WEST KOOTENAY

Over 50 vanished communities that include Cascade, Arrowhead, Poplar, Three Forks, Sandon, Brooklyn and others from the Arrow Lakes to the Lardeau, the Lower Columbia River to the Silvery Slocan. Until now most have lived only in newspaper files, government reports and memories of pioneers.

Includes over 80 historical and contemporary photos. Map. Four-color covers. 112 pages. $7.95

STAGECOACH AND STERNWHEEL DAYS IN THE CARIBOO AND CENTRAL B.C.

In 1863 the first stagecoach rumbled from Yale 400 miles northward to Barkerville. This well-illustrated book recreates stagecoach and sternwheel days when today's five-hour drive from Ashcroft to Prince George was "only a matter of four or five days."

Well illustrated with historical photos. 96 pages. $5.95

HISTORIC FRASER AND THOMPSON RIVER CANYONS

The Trans-Canada Highway from Vancouver to Kamloops offers scenery from mountains to sagebrush, wildlife from mountain goat to muskrat, vegetation from dogwood to cactus. Here is a mile-by-mile guide — including its colorful history.

Black and white and color photos plus map. 128 pages. $7.95

THE DEWDNEY TRAIL: British Columbia's Highway 3 from Hope to Fort Steele.
Built in 1865 over 400 miles from the Coast Mountains to the Rockies, this route is now paved Highway 3.

With over 100 photos, this route description includes wildlife, government campsites, communities and history. 160 pages. $9.95

An Explorer's Guide: MARINE PARKS OF B.C.
To tens of thousands of boaters, B.C.'s Marine Parks are as welcome and convenient as their popular highway equivalents. This guide includes anchorages and onshore facilities, trails, picnic areas, campsites, history and other information. In addition, it is profusely illustrated with color and black and white photos, maps and charts.

Informative reading for boat owners from runabouts to cabin cruisers. 200 pages. $12.95

GO FISHING WITH THESE BEST SELLING TITLES

HOW TO CATCH SALMON — BASIC FUNDAMENTALS
The most popular salmon book ever written. Information on trolling, rigging tackle, most productive lures, proper depths, salmon habits, how to play and net your fish, downriggers, where to find fish.
Sales over 120,000. 176 pages. $4.95

HOW TO CATCH SALMON — ADVANCED TECHNIQUES
The most comprehensive advanced salmon fishing book available. Over 200 pages crammed full of how-to tips and easy-to-follow diagrams. Covers all popular salmon fishing methods: mooching, trolling with bait, spoons and plugs, catching giant chinook, and much more.
A continuing best seller. 256 pages. $8.95

HOW TO CATCH CRABS: How popular is this book? This is the 10th printing. 114 pages. $3.50

HOW TO CATCH BOTTOMFISH: Revised and expanded. $4.95

HOW TO CATCH SHELLFISH: Updated 4th printing. 144 pages. $3.95

HOW TO CATCH TROUT by Lee Straight, one of Canada's top outdoorsmen. 144 pages. $4.95

HOW TO COOK YOUR CATCH: Cooking seafood on the boat, in a camper or at the cabin. 7th printing. 192 pages. $3.95

LIVING OFF THE SEA
Detailed techniques for catching crabs, prawn, shrimp, sole, cod and other bottomfish; oysters, clams and more. How to clean, fillet, shuck — in fact everything you need to know to enjoy the freshest seafood in the world.
Four-color covers and lots of helpful diagrams. 128 pages. $7.95

FLY FISH THE TROUT LAKES
with Jack Shaw
Professional outdoor writers describe the author as a man "who can come away regularly with a string when everyone else has been skunked." In this book, he shares over 40 years of studying, raising and photographing all forms of lake insects and the behaviour of fish to them.
Written in an easy-to-follow style. 96 pages. $7.95

Please send me the following books:

COPIES	TITLE	EACH	TOTAL
......	PIONEER DAYS IN BRITISH COLUMBIA - Volume One	$ 8.95	....
......	PIONEER DAYS IN BRITISH COLUMBIA - Volume Two	$ 8.95	....
......	PIONEER DAYS IN BRITISH COLUMBIA - Volume Three	$ 8.95	....
......	PIONEER DAYS IN BRITISH COLUMBIA - Volume Four	$ 8.95	....
......	WHITE SLAVES OF THE NOOTKA	$ 8.95	....
	LOWER MAINLAND BACKROADS:		
......	Volume One - Garibaldi to Lillooet, Bridge River Country	$ 9.95	....
......	Volume Two - The Fraser Valley	$ 2.95	....
......	Volume Three - Junction Country: Boston Bar to Clinton	$ 9.95	....
	OUTLAWS AND LAWMEN OF WESTERN CANADA -		
......	Volume One...	$ 7.95	....
	OUTLAWS AND LAWMEN OF WESTERN CANADA -		
......	Volume Two...	$ 7.95	....
	OUTLAWS AND LAWMEN OF WESTERN CANADA -		
......	Volume Three...	$ 9.95	....
......	B.C. PROVINCIAL POLICE STORIES: Mystery and Murder from the Files of Western Canada's First Lawmen	$ 7.95	....
......	THE DEATH OF ALBERT JOHNSON: Mad Trapper of Rat River	$ 7.95	....
......	FORT STEELE: Here History Lives	$ 9.95	....
......	TRAGEDIES OF THE CROWSNEST PASS	$ 6.95	....
......	THE BEST OF B.C. HIKING TRAILS	$ 9.95	....
......	GHOST TOWNS AND DROWNED TOWNS OF WEST		
......	KOOTENAY	$ 7.95	....
......	STAGECOACH AND STERNWHEEL DAYS	$ 5.95	....
......	HISTORIC FRASER AND THOMPSON RIVER CANYONS	$ 7.95	....
......	THE DEWDNEY TRAIL	$ 9.95	....
......	An Explorer's Guide: MARINE PARKS OF B.C.	$12.95	....
......	HOW TO CATCH SALMON - BASIC FUNDAMENTALS	$ 4.95	....
......	HOW TO CATCH SALMON - ADVANCED TECHNIQUES	$ 8.95	....
......	HOW TO CATCH CRABS	$ 3.50	....
......	HOW TO CATCH BOTTOMFISH	$ 4.95	....
......	HOW TO CATCH SHELLFISH	$ 3.95	....
......	HOW TO CATCH TROUT	$ 4.95	....
......	LIVING OFF THE SEA	$ 7.95	....
......	FLY FISH THE TROUT LAKES	$ 7.95	....

Total ....

Payment can be by Cheque or Money Order

HERITAGE HOUSE PUBLISHING COMPANY LTD.
Box 1228, Station A, Surrey, B.C. V3S 2B3

NAME (PLEASE PRINT)

ADDRESS

CITY   PROVINCE   POSTAL CODE

(ALL PRICES QUOTED ARE CURRENT AT TIME OF GOING TO PRESS.
HOWEVER, AS BOOKS ARE REPRINTED, PRICES MAY CHANGE.)